P.J. Emerson

FROM BELFAST TO THE BALKANS

WAS 'DEMOCRACY' PART OF THE PROBLEM?

D1553780

‡

Published by
THE DE BORDA INSTITUTE

*"A referendum mania ensued in Yugoslavia,
in which several other groups including the Albanians of Kosovo,
the Moslems of Sandžak, and the Serbs of Bosnia and Herzegovina,
in addition to the Serbs in Croatia and the Albanians in Macedonia,
[voted] on their respective political status."*

The Referendum on Independence in Bosnia and Herzegovina,
The Commission on Security and Co-operation in Europe, 1992, p 8.

The author wishes to give especial mention to the Agency for Personal Service Overseas, (APSO), which is part of *Irish Aid*, the government's official development assistance programme. APSO thrice sent him to Bosnia as part of the Irish contingent of international election observers, and later funded his 1999 'special service' deployment to Sarajevo as a political observer to the OSCE.

FROM BELFAST TO THE BALKANS

WAS 'DEMOCRACY' A PART OF THE PROBLEM?

ISBN 0 9506028 7 6

Published by
THE DE BORDA INSTITUTE

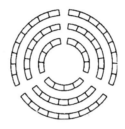

THE DE BORDA INSTITUTE
36 Ballysillan Road
Belfast BT14 7QQ
pemerson@deborda.freeserve.co.uk
www.members.tripod.com/~deBorda/
http://members.tripod.co.uk/deBordaInstitute

Those who use any information contained in this book
are asked to give all due credits.

This book has received support from the Cultural Traditions Programme of the Community Relations
Council, which aims to encourage acceptance and understanding of cultural diversity.
The views expressed do not necessarily reflect those of the NI Community Relations Council.

Typeset by the author.

Printed by Noel Murphy (Printing), Belfast

PRONUNCIATION NOTES.

Serbo-Croat is now known by three separate names: Bosnian, Croatian and Serbian. It is, however, just the one language, albeit in two scripts and more than two dialects. In the text which follows, we have confined ourselves to the Latin script, which differs from English in a number of ways. The letter *j*, for example, softens the adjoining one, and certain letters - *c, d, s* and *z* - have their accented or soft forms, as follows:

letter		written	pronounced	examples from the text written		pronounced
c	=	č or ć	ch as in 'church'	Andrić	=	Andrich
				Bihać	=	Bihach
				četnik	=	chetnik
				Kljujić	=	Klyuich
				Kučan	=	Kuchan
				Izetbegović	=	Izetbegovich
				Marković	=	Markovich
				Mihailović	=	Mihailovich
				Panić	=	Panich
				Pavelić	=	Pavelich
				Raznatović	=	Raznatovich
				Tapić	=	Tapich
d	=	đ	dj			Tudjman
s	=	š	sh as in 'shoe'	Dušan	=	Dushan
				Poplašen	=	Poplashen
				Priština	=	Prishtina
				Šešelj	=	Sheshel
				ustaša	=	ustasha
				Višegrad	=	Vishegrad
z	=	ž	zh or j as in 'Jane'	Draža	=	Drazha
				Goražde	=	Gorazhde
				Ilidža	=	Ilidzha
				Sandžak	=	Sandzhak
				Željko	=	Zhel'ko
				Žepa	=	Zhepa

Sometimes, of course, two soft letters can occur in the one word:

Milošević	=	Miloshevich
Karadžić	=	Karadzhich

The hard c, by the way, unlike its English equivalent, has one fixed sound:

c	ts as in 'bats'	Srebrenica =	Srebrenitsa

so finally, the most important word of all:

šlivovic	=	shlivovits.

NB   Kosova is sometimes spelt Kosovo; the former spelling is preferred by the Albanians, the latter by the Serbs. This text uses both.

CONTENTS

ABBREVIATIONS

BRITISH & IRISH	BALKAN	OTHER	
		AMS	additional member system
		AV	alternative vote
	B-H		Bosnia and Herzegovina
DUP			Democratic Unionist Party
		EC	European Community
		EU	European Union
	FRY		Federal Republic of Yugoslavia
	HDZ		Croatian Democratic Union
		IDEA	Institute for Democracy and Electoral Assistance
		IMF	International Monetary Fund
IRSP			Irish Republican Socialist Party
	KLA		Kosova Liberation Army
	MBO		Moslem Bosniac Organisation
		MMP	multi-member proportional
		NATO	North Atlantic Treaty Organisation
	NHI		New Croatian Initiative
NI			Northern Ireland
NILP			NI Labour Party
	NWG		National Working Group
	OHR		Office of the High Representative
	OSCE		Organisation for Security and Co-operation in Europe
		PR	proportional representation
PUP			Progressive Unionist Party
		QBS	quota Borda system
	RS		*Republika Srpska*
RSF			Republican SF
	SDA		Party of Democratic Action
SDLP			Social Democratic and Labour Party
	SDP		Social Democratic Party
	SDS		Serbian Democratic Party
SF			Sinn Féin
	SRS		Serbian Radical Party
		STV	single transferable vote
		UDI	unilateral declaration of independence
UDP			Ulster Democratic Party
UK			United Kingdom
UKUP			UK Unionist Party
		UN	United Nations
	UNPROFOR		UN Protection Force
UPNI			Unionist Party of NI
		USA	United States of America
		USSR	Union of Soviet Socialist Republics
UUP			Ulster Unionist Party
UVF			Ulster Volunteer Force

GLOSSARY

For words Yugoslavian, see below; for terms psephological, see overleaf.

Bosnians   or *Bosniaks*. The inhabitants of Bosnia, most of whom are Slavs, and many of these identify with one of three religions: Catholic, Moslem and Orthodox.

četniks   This was a term given to those under Mihailović who (sometimes) fought against Hitler. The name was also used to describe the rebel Bosnian Serbs under Karadžić.

Croats   Originally, the Croats (like the Serbs) were a pagan Slav tribe, from somewhere near the Caspian Sea. They arrived in the Balkans round about the 6th century, and many were converted to Catholicism some two centuries later.

Entity   The term devised as part of the Dayton Agreement to describe the two parts of Bosnia-Herzegovina. One is *Republika Srpska*, the other is the Moslem-Croat Federation.

FRY   Now consists of only Serbia and Montenegro.

Illyrians   The earliest known inhabitants of present day Albania and parts of Yugoslavia.

Kosova/o   This was an autonomous republic in Serbia from 1974 until Milošević re-incorporated the area back into Serbia proper in 1989.

krajina   The word is derived from the Serbo-Croat *'kraj'* meaning 'region' or 'end', and there were three such frontier zones in Croatia, where Serbs were settled to defend the Austro-Hungarian border from Ottoman incursions.

nation   A nation is defined as a group of people of one ethnicity, whatever that is. In old-fashioned theory, one nation inhabits, or used to inhabit, one state.

OSCE   The OSCE was born of the Helsinki conference in 1975. This unarmed organisation helps to defuse conflicts, assist democratisation processes and administer elections.

Republika Srpska   One of the entities in B-H.

Sandžak   This is an area of south-west Serbia, although originally it also included part of Montenegro, and was an old administrative region of the Ottoman Empire. The majority of inhabitants in the *Sandžak* are both Moslem *and* Serb, who unfortunately regard themselves as *either* Moslem *or* Serb. Again, they are all Slav.

Serbs   See Croats, above. To-day, many Serbs belong to the Orthodox faith.

state   A state is a supposedly sovereign administrative unit, in which live peoples of one or more nationality.

ustaša   Croatian fascists during WWII, who re-emerged in the 1990s.

Vlahs/Vlachs   A distinctive ethnic group who date back to at least the tenth century. They appear to have been semi-nomadic herds people, deft in their horsemanship.

Vojvodina   Like Kosova, Vojvodina was an autonomous region of Serbia, gained by the latter at the end of WWI. It is a very mixed region, with many Hungarians and others.

Yugoslavia   The word, meaning *"southern Slavia"*, was first coined in 1848.

AMS Additional member system. A one-vote version of MMP (see below). When the latter system is used, the voters have a little more choice, so many voters vote (tactically) for a larger party in the first vote, and for a smaller one in the second.

AV Alternative vote. When the single transferable vote is used either in decision-making or in the election of only one representative, it is called AV.

Borda The Borda count or Borda preferendum can be used as a decision-making process, or in elections either by itself or incorporated into QBS. The voter awards points to one, some or all the options/candidates listed, and the option/candidates with the most points is/are the winner/s.

Condorcet Another multi-option decision-making voting procedure. Voters cast preferences for all the options, and these are then considered in pairs, to see which option wins most, or even all, of these pairings.

consociational majority voting A decision-making methodology which divides society into two or more (ethnic or geographical) groups, and in which all votes are subject to a majority verdict in both or all of these constituencies.

d'Hondt A little mathematical formula by which to award seats in a PR election. Each party's totals are divided by a set of divisors - 1, 2, 3, 4... - and seats are awarded to the biggest totals, herebelow shown underlined. The system favours the bigger parties.

 Imagine a five-seater in which 100 voters give party A 60, B 40 and C 0 votes. We first divide these totals by 1, 2, 3... to get {<u>60</u>, <u>40</u>, 0}, {<u>30</u>, <u>20</u>, 0} and {<u>20</u>, 17, 0}, so to give party A 3 seats and B 2. Fair enough, you might say.

 If, however, A, B and C win 50, 30 and 20 votes, and we divide these by 1, 2, 3... we get {<u>50</u>, <u>30</u>, <u>20</u>}, {<u>25</u>, 15, 10}{<u>17</u>, 10, 7}, so seats go to A 3, B 1 and C 1, which maybe isn't so fair! Which is why there are other formulae; see Emerson, 1998.

first-past-the-post or plurality voting (see below). It is used in many Anglo-Saxon democracies, 68 countries in all, and often leads to two-party systems of government.

MMP Multi-member proportional. The voter has two votes, the first to elect a single representative in a local constituency, as in first-past-the-post; and the second to choose a top-up representative in a PR-List election in either a few regional or one national constituency. This element tries to ensure overall proportionality. The system is used in Germany and New Zealand, and is sometimes (mistakenly) called AMS.

plurality voting In any two-option/candidate vote, the winner is that option/candidate which/who gains the majority; in a similar vote where there are more than two - i.e., a *plurality* of - options/candidates, the winner is the one with a majority, or maybe only the largest minority!

PR There are two basic types of PR: the first is an (open or) closed list system, in which the voter is able to vote for (one candidate of) one party; the second is STV or QBS, where the voter can express a number of preferences for several candidates, of one or more parties, and/or perhaps of none.

QBS The quota Borda system is a pluralist PR electoral system in which a candidate's success depends either on the quota and/or on his/her Borda count, i.e., his/her level of support throughout the constituency. It is an inclusive electoral system.

STV Single transferable vote. This allows the voter to vote for one or some options/candidates, of one or some parties, and a preference which is not used because that option/candidate has already been (elected or) eliminated is transferred to the voter's subsequent preference.

CAST OF CHARACTERS

Ahern, Bertie — Leader of Fianna Fail and Irish *Taoiseach,* 1997-

Arkan — Željko Raznatović, a Serbian war lord turned politician, responsible for 'ethnic cleansing' in Vukovar in the Croatian war, and in Bijeljina during the Bosnian war.

Blair, Tony — Leader of the Labour Party and British Prime Minister, 1997 -

Boban, Mate — A more extreme Bosnian Croat, who replaced Kljujić.

Broz, Josip (Tito) — Leader of the Partisans, and leader of Yugoslavia, 1945-80.

Carrington, Lord David — A former NATO Secretary General who then became the EC's negotiator in the Balkans in 1991.

Churchill, Sir Winston — Wartime British premier.

Dzugashvili, Joseph (Stalin) — A bolshevik who, as leader of the Soviet Union from 1924 till his death in 1953, was responsible for the deaths of at least 24 million in the labour camps of Siberia.

Ferdinand, Franz — The Archduke and heir to the Austro-Hungarian throne, who was assassinated in Sarajevo in 1914.

Izetbegović, Alija — President of Bosnia-Herzegovina since 1990.

Gorbachev, Mikhail — Leader of the USSR, 1985-91.

Hitler, Adolf — Nazi leader in Germany, from 1933-45. Like Stalin, he too caused millions to die in death camps.

Karadžić, Radovan — Leader of the rebel Bosnian Serbs from 1990, and now an indicted war criminal, still at large somewhere in Bosnia.

Kljujić, Stjepan — Moderate Bosnian Croat leader, pushed out by Tudjman

Kučan, Milan — Slovene Communist Party leader who then became Slovenia's first president.

Major, John — The rather weak British Prime Minister who succeeded Thatcher in 1990.

Marković, Ante — Last Federal Prime Minister, 1989-91, and leader of Reform League.

Mihailović, Draža — Leader of the *četniks* during WWII, and executed in 1946.

Milošević, Slobodan — Leader in Serbia from 1987. He initially came to power through the ranks of the Communist Party but then, like so many others, (not least Tudjman in Croatia), he managed to consolidate his power 'democratically'.

Mowlam, Mo	NI Secretary of State, 1997-9.
O'Bradaigh, Ruairi	Leader of RSF.
Owen, Lord David	Former British Foreign Secretary who was chosen to succeed Lord Carrington as the EC's negotiator, though why should a Briton, with the UK so unsuccessful in NI, be considered an expert on ethnic conflict resolution?
Paisley, Rev Ian, (RIP)	Leader of the DUP.
Pavelić, Ante	Leader of the fascist Croatian state in WWII, and yet another dictator who used a concentration camp to pursue his policy of 'ethnic cleansing'.
Poplašen, Nikola	Leader (under Šešelj) of the SRS in Bosnia, and 'winner' of the 1998 *RS* presidential elections... but only because of the rotten electoral system.
Raznatović, Željko	see Arkan.
Reagan, Ronald	President of the USA, 1986-94.
Roosevelt, F.D.	Wartime US president, until his death in 1945.
Rugova, Ibrahim	The president of the Kosovar Association of Writers who became the leader of the 'Democratic League of Kosovo' in 1989 and the elected president of Kosova in 1992.
Šešelj, Vojislav	Like Arkan, another warlord. Leader of the extreme SRS in Serbia (and Bosnia).
Stepinac, Alojzije	Roman Catholic Cardinal and head of the church in Croatia during WWII, where many members of the clergy openly sided with the Croatian fascists or *ustaša*.
Thatcher, Margaret	UK Prime Minister from 1979-90.
Tudjman, Franjo	President of Croatia from 1992, but not for much longer, they say.
Tvrtko, King	The Ban or ruler of Bosnia from 1353, who was then crowned as king in 1377 and reigned until his death in 1391.
Westendorp, Carlos	The High Representative in Bosnia and, as such, the person ultimately responsible for the administration of that country, if and when the joint presidency of one Bosniak, one Croat and one Serb doesn't manage to agree, which is always.
Yeltsin, Boris	Whether ill or inebriated, President of the Russian Federation from 1991 to 1999.

FOREWORD

Some years ago, I arrived in Moscow looking for a man who, I'd been told, would be able to give me some advice as to how I could get my bike on a train down to the then Soviet Republic of Georgia.

My first line of enquiry brought me to Conor O'Cleary, formerly Moscow Correspondent of The Irish Times.

"Do you happen to know where I can find a man called Emerson?" I asked. *"Peter Emerson?"*

"Yes," said Conor. *"As a matter of fact, I do. He's in today's* 'Pravda', *telling the Russians how to run their country."*

It's a brave man that would do that and as I got to know Peter, I realised telling people what to do is not, in fact, his style. This is not a man who thunders about his pet subject - democracy and its many failings - pinning you to the wall of the bar as he sets out his thesis on the inadequacies of most voting systems and promoting his own - the De Borda system. No, Peter's approach is much more subtle than that. He simply demonstrates the way in which the either/or system of voting is such a poor servant of the people - the demos of democracy. (See page 36 for an analysis of how first past the winning post democracy best serves those already in power, vide Tudjman's Croatia and Thatcher's Britain.)

* * * * * * * *

After Moscow, our paths diverged and our next significant meeting was, unexpectedly, on a street in Sarajevo. We had both been sent to different parts of Bosnia as part of an international team of election observers.

This was not Peter's first visit to the Balkans. He chose the bitterly cold winter of 1992/93 to travel around war torn Bosnia - pedalling serenely through military checkpoints, waved on by soldiers who, seeing a bearded man on a ramshackle bike, mistook him for a local. His knowledge of the Russian language enabled him to talk to Serbs, Croatians and Bosniaks and at one checkpoint, a soldier quizzed him about his Belfast origins: father Irish protestant, mother English catholic. *"Ah,"* said the soldier, *"a true Yugoslav,"* and offered him a glass of *šlivovic* - the perfect breakfast on a winter's morning.

* * * * * * * *

In *"**From Belfast to the Balkans**"*, Peter examines a system of democracy which forces punters to come down on one side or the other. To vote 'yes-or-no'. To chose 'black-or-white'. No place for those who want to vote: 'Yes, but'. It must be all or nothing in a system which he labels *"a two-option question for a multi-option problem."*

What he would like to see - and he is not alone - is a system which gives everyone a voice no matter how small that voice is or how few people it represents. Drawing inspiration from De Borda himself, the system ensures that *"everyone contributes to the outcome of a dispute and in such a way that no one faction wins everything but (almost) everyone wins something."* Sometimes, a vote is avoided altogether while all parties try to reach a consensus. (I have seen this work well in South Africa and not so well in Northern Ireland.)

But is this idealism raising its troublesome head here, perhaps you'll ask? How practical are these procedures? How will we manage if we don't have big powerful party machines running the show? If we don't have the support of the big international players?

For support, read intervention by the US known, euphemistically, as the international community. *"For years, Reagan and company,"* the author writes, *"were trying to persuade the Republic of Ireland to join NATO, as a* quid pro quo *for eventual unity."*

Fast forward from the Reagan years to 11.20 am on December 1st, 1999 when the Republic of Ireland signed the NATO-led Partnership for Peace agreement while, later in the day, Queen Elizabeth II signed the devolution order which formally transferred power from Westminster to the Northern Ireland Assembly. Coincidence? Or a *quid pro quo* system that has precious little to do with democracy?

* * * * * * * *

Winston Churchill said that though democracy was a poor thing it was all we had. A jaundiced point of view but perhaps understandable, given his experience of the two-party system.

Had he been able to read this excellent book, he might well have developed a different point of view.

Mary Russell
2.2.2000
Dublin

INTRODUCTION

By accident of birth, I am the child of a mixed marriage, mixed, that is, by religion and nationality as well. My elder brother, born in Belfast, lives in England and thinks he is British. My younger sister, born in England but now domiciled in Dublin, thinks not. And I too am *"ethnically unclean"*, the perfect pedigree for anyone wishing to live in Northern Ireland.

My mother was never fond of this place, wartime memories and that sort of thing, so when I decided to come over here, I said (and I meant it), Oh don't worry, Mum; it's only for a year. That was in 1975, but then I changed my mind and, with just the occasional break, I've been here ever since. Initially, I said nothing, and I just listened. Six months later, on visiting a friend of a friend on the Malone Road, I realised that some of the locals knew even less than I. Thus I came to think that even a minority of one might have something to say. But first, I had to cross and re-cross the peace-line.

In 1975, I was still very much the practising Catholic. I therefore went to work in a Protestant youth club, on the Crumlin Road. When one of the lads was killed in a brawl, I did the obvious thing and went to his funeral, even though it was a Protestant paramilitary service. Not that many Catholics went drinking in the Loyalist Club, either, (but once they heard I was of the other foot, they decided my custom was no longer welcome).

The real proof of my 'street cred' came a little later. Sectarian tension in the club was often quite high, not least because of the cross-community contacts I promoted. On this particular evening, I locked up the youth club as usual and returned home on foot. Passing one back alley, I noticed a frightening bunch of young men, a UVF gang, coming in my direction. I ran the rest of the way home, locked the door and barricaded myself in. Only later did I learn it had actually been sent out for my protection!

We actually managed to do quite a lot of cross-community work, especially in the summer months, and on one occasion, I was taking a minibus load of kids to the beach. A little four-year old was behind me, and if a child is old enough to ask questions, they're surely old enough to hear the answers. What's your name? Where do you live? Do you go to church? Which one? And finally, which brought a tear to my eye: Then why aren't you hitting me?

* * * * * * * *

From the youth club I progressed to community work, on the peace line in North Belfast. The army, of course, was everywhere, in landrovers and sometimes on foot patrols. More especially in nationalist areas, they used to stop the pedestrian and ask a few questions: name, age, sex, that sort of thing. On just such an occasion, I answered both simply and politely, but with the awfully English accent I've inherited from my birth. He wrote all the answers down, as a good soldier would, unthinking... but when he finished he did think. How on earth could a guy like this, unarmed and unabashed, walk round the streets of Catholic Ardoyne with impunity. What followed was not a question, but a statement of incredulity: you're fucking English! Both 'verb' and adjective were inaccurate.

At about this time, in a 1977 letter to the local press, I asked a question myself: why don't we use multi-option voting instead of this divisive majority vote? And I've been at it ever since. Initially, it was just a theory, but in 1986, it was all put into practice. Under the auspices of the New Ireland Group, I organised what we called the *"People's Conventions"*. The first was attended by over two hundred persons, and they included members of various political parties, everything from Sinn Féin to Ulster Unionists, and even Ulster Clubs! It was, if you like, an experiment in consensus. A multi-option debate was followed by a multi-option vote, and it worked; we found a compromise.

THE BALKANS

My knowledge of the Balkans does not go back quite so far, but I have managed to gain a fair impression from a number of experiences, some of which are linked directly to Belfast. My first visit was in 1990, when I cycled from Moscow to Tirana, a trip which passed through Romania, Bulgaria, Macedonia and Albania. Six months on a bicycle, I thought, was enough, so I gave the bike to my hosts in the Albanian capital and came home, by bus from Tirana, by foot across the border - Albania was still pretty well cut off in those days - and by train across Montenegro and Serbia.

One guy I met in a little village, not far from Skopje, invited me in for the night, as people often do to cold and damp cyclists in this part of the world. He was a Macedonian and, over a glass of *rekiya*, the local brew, he suggested I call in to see his brother in the city. The latter called himself a Serb.

It was not a typical cross-section of Skopje society which I encountered in a bar one day, for they were, as it happened, all men. No surprises there! But I was invited over, more drinks were ordered, and the introductions started: I'm a Montenegrin, said one; I'm a Serb, rejoined another; I'm a Bosnian, I'm a Macedonian; they were all there, enjoying their differences, and (unwittingly perhaps) confirming their similarities.

The politicians, however, were arguing. Well, that's what politicians do, you might say. And in Serbia, they were arguing about the economy... again, as always. The trouble is, very few politicians understand the economy, not least because most economists don't either.

Therefore, in order to compete with each other, various 'leaders' were resorting to something that they could understand: nationalism. And on matters which were nevertheless economic, each was trying to 'out-Serbify' the other. It was, I felt at the time, an incredibly dangerous game. I did not realise, of course, and nor I suspect did they, just exactly how dangerous it was.

In October 1991, back in Belfast, I organised a further conference on decision-making.[1] It too was attended by members of various political parties, and they included some fairly senior activists of both Sinn Féin and the Ulster Unionist Party, not to mention Alliance, Fianna Fáil, Fine Gael, Green Party, SDLP and so on.

If nothing else, Northern Ireland is a pretty good laboratory for those involved in conflict resolution. On this occasion, the participants used a (computerised) multi-option voting procedure - the Borda preferendum - and again, it worked. The conference was also attended by a Bosnian, Petar Radji-Histić. This was *before* the war in Bosnia, (although after the outbreak of hostilities in Croatia), and we tried to say, please, don't use a simple, two-option referendum in Bosnia. Six months later, in March 1992, they did exactly that. Within days, Bosnia was at war.

* * * * * * * *

Just as the bloody atrocities in Vukovar had shocked the world during the conflict in Croatia, so too the summer months revealed even worse events in Bosnia. There was systematic ethnic cleansing in Bijeljina, for example, and concentration camps like Omarska. Warnings of even greater sufferings in the approaching months of winter were commonplace.

Given the apparent disinterest of so many western governments, and given the numerous parallels between the conflict there and our own here, I decided to go to Bosnia, if but to say on my return to Northern Ireland, majoritarianism does not work there either. So it was that I resolved, firstly, to learn some Serbo-Croat, and secondly, to go in winter.

In December 1992, nine months into the war, I arrived at Sarajevo airport, care of an UNPROFOR Hercules relief flight, piloted by officers from the Luftwaffe.[2] The city was under siege. The temperature the night before was 16 below. It was cold, dark, and misty, and only the occasional candle from behind a polythene 'window' tried to pierce the freezing gloom. The streets were virtually empty, and gunfire was frequent, now a machine gun, now a heavier shell, over there, over here.

There was only one place to stay, they said, the infamous Holiday Inn. With two other journalists, we made our way to this hotel and asked for a room. The receptionist, wrapped in a blanket, sat in the corner with a piece of paper and a candle. No electricity, no water, nothing. How much? we asked. $70, all in. All in? Oh never mind, we'll take it, one will use the bed and two will sleep on the floor, but just the one room, please. Fine, he replied, that's still $70 a head. So we bid farewell, and disappeared into the Sarajevo night.

---

1   *"The Other Talks"*, held in the Mandela Hall of Queen's University, again under the auspices of the New Ireland Group.

2   Interestingly enough, the German Bundestag only took the decision to allow its armed forces personnel to serve abroad in July 1993.

In January, after also visiting Bihać, I set off from Zagreb and cycled just a little illegally into northern Bosnia and to Banja Luka (where I picked up my *'odobrenje'*, see pp 74-5). From there I came through the corridor[3] to Belgrade, before returning in March via Zvornik, Pale, Sarajevo and Mostar to Split. On numerous occasions, I was asked why I was in Bosnia, and not least because people thought I was earning a lot of money. When they heard that I was there at my own expense, they were more sympathetic; and if any doubts still remained, it all became clear when I told them I was from Belfast.

* * * * * * * *

Crossing the front line from Pale into Sarajevo airport was fairly dangerous for a cyclist, so on my way out again, I got a lift. We went from the city centre, through three check-points and over the no man's land 'frontier', to Serb-held Ilidža. The bombed out houses and intermittent sniper fire were proof enough that a war was going on. A few miles later, we came to a second front line, where there was hardly anything at all: this was like going from Belgium to France. So from Sarajevo under siege, with no water and *nema ništa* (nothing), I came to the central Bosnian town of Kiseljak, with bars, fags and Croatian flags, with Croatian police, and Croatian money, and Croatian everything. War was worse than cruel.

* * * * * * * *

My next visit to Bosnia, in September 1996, was as an elections supervisor for the OSCE, the Organisation (they joked in Sarajevo) to Secure Clinton's Election. The chosen electoral system, as we shall see in Chapter 5, was not good, and nor was the count; at least the latter was better one year later, when I was back again for the *Republika Srpska (RS)* presidential contest, and again in 1998, for the second post-Dayton general election.

In January 1999, I returned as a political adviser to the OSCE, to spend a month in the country, (travelling by bus on this occasion), to talk with all sorts: journalists, human rights activists, politicians, electoral commissioners and academics. Finally, within days of the end of NATO's war against Serbia, I attended a seminar in Konjic and then - my spare bike is in Sarajevo - cycled across the Sandžak to Kosovo, and back again via Montenegro.

CONCULSION

I met some lovely Serbs. Would people in Ireland be so kind? asked one Belgrade lady who took me in for the night in her parent's village in Montenegro. I also met some who were not so nice. Yet even the most bigoted, who drown you with nonsensical arguments and blatantly racist distortions, still buy you a beer.

---

3   The corridor was the narrow strip of land linking the western half of *Republika Srpska* under Banja Luka, with the eastern section under Pale. The 'enemy' was on both sides, the Croats to the north and the combined Moslem/Croat forces to the south. Mortar fire was again frequent.

In the course of my travels, I also encountered some lovely and not so lovely Croats, Bosnians and Albanians (to put them in my own chronological order). In the same way, there are some lovely folk of all sorts in Northern Ireland. It ill behoves any to demonise any one ethnic group in its entirety, yet that is what tends to happen, most certainly in international diplomacy when sanctions are deployed or war is declared; but it also happens in our internal politics, when we vote *for* some and *against,* it would seem, everybody else. There is, then, something fundamentally wrong in our basic democratic structures.

* * * * * * * *

Ireland, by virtue of its geography, is insular, and for years and years, many thought the problems in Northern Ireland were unique. Cyprus, to name just one conflict, suggested otherwise of course, but since the collapse of the Berlin Wall, most now accept that our problems are indeed reflected elsewhere, especially in that other European conflict in the Balkans. It is, needless to say, very much more complicated over there, but there are some parallels. And if there are parallels in the problems, there are bound to be some similarities in any sensible solutions.

THE BOOK

In the pages which follow, we discuss these likenesses. In Chapter 1, we talk in general terms of the way people try to resolve conflicts by using a majority vote referendum, yet in many instances, such a methodology only exacerbates that conflict. Chapter 2 moves from the general to the particular, and compares the relatively small conflict in Northern Ireland with the huge yet perhaps surprisingly similar problems in the Balkans.

To resolve these problems in a win-or-lose process is obviously unwise; accordingly, in Chapter 3, we look at the worst two-option process: war. And after examining our respective electoral systems in Chapter 4, we criticise the second two-option decision-making process - majoritarianism - and not least because it so often provokes the first.

Finally, in Chapter 6, we conclude on a more optimistic note and take a look at the current problem in both conflict zones, the implementations of the respective peace processes. It is, let's face it, a much nicer problem.

And now, at last, a word of thanks: to Melita Kalčić who checked my translation; to Mark McCann who computerised my maps; and to all the members of The de Borda Institute committee, who have helped to rationalise my thoughts.

Peter Emerson
Belfast
1.11.99

The Former and Future Yugoslavia

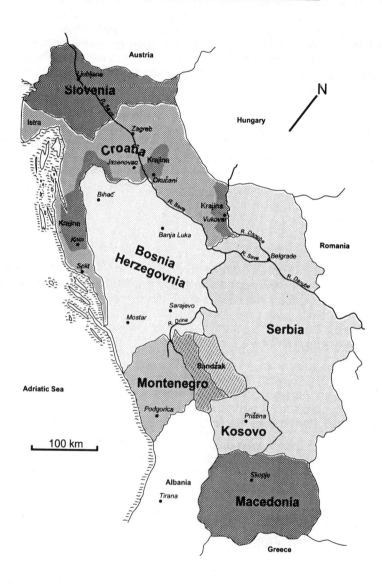

Bosnia and Herzegovina

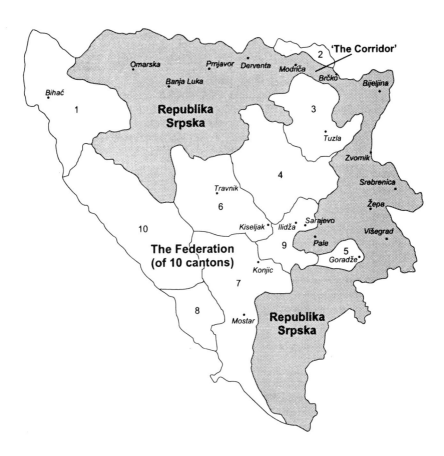

'The Corridor'

Omarska

Prnjavor   Derventa   Modriča

Banja Luka

Brčko

Bijeljina

Bihać

1

Republika
Srpska

2

3

Tuzla

Zvornik

4

Srebrenica

Travnik

Žepa

6

Sarajevo

10

Kiseljak   Ilidža

Višegrad

The Federation
(of 10 cantons)

9   Pale

5

Goradže

Konjic

7

8

Mostar

Republika
Srpska

CHRONOLOGY

1941		Nazis bomb Belgrade, just as the Austrians bombed in 1914.
1945		End of WWII, start of Cold War. Tito takes over in Yugoslavia, with many executions.
1948		Tito breaks with Stalin and becomes a friend of the West, as any other anti-Moscow communist was to do later on; e.g., Ceauşescu.
1968		USSR enters Czechoslovakia and suppresses the Czech spring.
1969		The 'troubles' in Northern Ireland.
1971		Tudjman and other 'nationalists' protest in Zagreb; this does *not* deserve to be called 'the Croatian spring'.
1974		Tito's new constitution for a power-sharing Federation.
1975		Helsinki Act; all countries recognise i) all borders, including Yugoslavia's; and ii) the right of peoples to self-determination.
1980		Tito dies.
1985		Gorbachev comes to power in Moscow and initiates 'perestroika'; end of Cold War; Anglo-Irish Agreement.
1987		Milošević takes control in Belgrade.
1988		First ethnic conflict in Soviet Union in Nagorno-Karabakh.
1990		First multi-party elections in the various Republics of Yugoslavia; nationalism takes over.
1991	Jan	Gorbachev sends troops into Lithuania; West now switches to Yeltsin, so to support the break-up of USSR, and therefore (sic) of Yugoslavia as well.
	Mar	Anti-government demonstration in Belgrade.
	Jun	Slovenia and Croatia declare independence. 10-day war in Slovenia.
	Aug	War in Croatia.
1992	Jan	West recognises Croatia and Slovenia, but not Bosnia.
	Mar	Referendum, and then war, in B-H.
1993	May	Vance-Owen Plan rejected.
1994		First ceasefire in NI.
1995	May	Tudjman overruns the Okučani *Krajina*.
	Jul	Karadžić executes thousands in Srebrenica and Žepa.
	Aug	Tudjman (and US) ethnically cleanse the Knin *Krajina*. Yet another bomb in Sarajevo's market place; the West responds, at last, under a NATO rather than a UN command.
	Nov	Dayton.
1996	Apr	First act of force by KLA.
1997		Albania in chaos after pyramid crisis.
	Oct	Montenegro's new president opposes Milošević.
1999	Feb	Rambouillet.
	Mar	NATO bombs Belgrade.
	Jun	The undeclared war ends after Russia re-negotiates terms.

CHAPTER 1

THE PROBLEM

*"Why should I be a minority in your state
when you can be a minority in mine?"*

Vladimir Gligorov[1]

I write these words with a degree of urgency. East Timor held a referendum on 1st Sept. 1999. As a result, the peoples of Aceh and Ambon are also asking for polls on independence. Irian Jaya may well be next. Indonesia consists of over 3,000 inhabited islands. Does each have the right to self-determination?

I know very little about Indonesia. Of course it was wrong for the Indonesian authorities to occupy East Timor by force. It may also be wrong for such a huge country to be run from one centralised capital. The purpose of this book, however, is simply to say that whenever there arises a controversial question of sovereignty, the resolution thereof should not be via a divisive, two-option, yes-or-no referendum.

Some are already calling Indonesia *"Asia's Yugoslavia"*.

Other nation-states are faced with a similar problem. Should Dagestan have a referendum? Some residents there have already taken up arms against Russia, supposedly in a bid for independence. But if Chechnya and then Dagestan go, what follows? Tartarstan? Karelia? Will Yeltsin allow the entire Russian Federation to fall apart? Such an outcome might or might not be desirable. The question, however, is this: will the process be peaceful?

Or take China. Many (including this author) would argue that Tibet should regain her independence. If, however, the instrument by which that policy is enacted is to be the referendum, then maybe there is no hope at all: China, after all, has flooded Tibet with its own peoples. Even if such a poll could work in Tibet, what would then happen in other parts of China? Or in India, where some are already demanding a referendum in Kashmir? Or, on a smaller scale, in Canada, in the province of Quebec? And to this problem we shall return.

The point is this. A people (whatever that is) should not be allowed to determine itself on the basis of only a majority of itself. If one lot wants to separate from another, there should be an amicable divorce. The Czechoslovak example is often quoted, although that was not as amicable as some try to paint it. So we'll mention that one later on as well.

---

1   A political theorist, quoted in Woodward, p 108. He is no relation, by the way, to his namesake, Kiro Gligorov, the President of Macedonia.

In the pages which follow, we will discuss and compare the use of the two-option vote in just two of the conflicts which have come to plague the closing years of the 20th century: Belfast and the Balkans. There was little amicable in either. Majority rule was always (not *the* but) *a* cause of the problems in Northern Ireland, and little wonder that the border poll referendum in 1973, even though it was meant to bring peace, did nothing of the sort!

Sadly, the lessons were unlearned, and at the insistence of the European Commission/Union, EC or EU, the chosen methodology for the resolution of all the sovereignty disputes in Yugoslavia was the same, simplistic referendum.

The result, as they say, is history, and it was best summed up by *Oslobodjenje*, Sarajevo's now legendary newspaper: *"all the wars in the former Yugoslavia started with a referendum"*.[2] At that time, they were referring to the wars in Slovenia, Croatia and Bosnia; but, as I shall argue in Chapter 5, the war in Kosova was also caused, in large part, by (the prospects of) a referendum.

* * * * * * * *

As we all know, many books have been published on the problems of Northern Ireland, and numerous works now discuss the break-up of Yugoslavia. For reasons which can only be called extraordinary, however, although some do complain about the use of the simple majority vote or referendum, very few mention alternative democratic decision-making processes, let alone identify a voting methodology of conflict prevention.

The right of self-determination is a major cause of controversy. The unionists claimed it for the six counties of 'Ulster'. The nationalists wanted it for all 32 counties. Yet both sets of antagonists failed to question the procedure; both continued to believe in the second most primitive form of decision-making ever invented, this straight majority vote; and when they failed to get what they wanted, one or both resorted to the first most primitive form of decision-making, that other two-option decision-making process, violence.

Similarly, in Yugoslavia, alternative decision-making methodologies were seldom if ever on the agenda. Many authors have questioned the right of self-determination. Many quote such fine statements as the 1993 Vienna Declaration of Programme for Action: *"All peoples shall have the right to self-determination. By virtue of that right, they freely determine their political status."* And many then ask that pretty fundamental question: 'what is a people?'

Well, 'they' might be the nation, those of a particular ethnic group who, over the years, have increased and multiplied, and whose present day borders may not be so appropriate. 'They' might be a different 'they', namely, only those of that nationality who now live there, no matter how illogical their

---

2   *Op cit*, 7.2.99, p 11. *"... su svi ratovi u bivšoj Yugoslaviji počeli nekim referendumom"*.

present borders, or how sad the historical origin of such frontiers. 'They' (the people) might include other lots as well, namely all of those who now live within these existing borders, whoever these people are or whatever their ethnicity. Or lastly, 'they' might be those who have fought and won some bloody war! These four principles (sic) of self-determination - the historicist, democratic, Helsinki and realist principles[3] - are often discussed at length. The question of *who* votes, yes, is often heard: will it be those of a nation, or those in a state? But the question *how?* Hardly anyone questions that. In most cases, it is just assumed there will be a simple majority vote.

In a few places of relative peace, governments sometimes use multi-option (majority or) plurality voting.[4] Where there is the possibility of conflict, however, if there is a vote at all, they always use the most divisive form, the simple, two-option majority vote. It is a cause of war. This book is written in order to discuss, with a view to removing, that cause.

* * * * * * * *

There may, of course, be other causes of conflict within the democratic process. Under the conditions laid down in most democratic systems, a politician needs the support of only 'his own' in order to get elected and/or to get his policies adopted. This would suggest that before the ambitious think of the good of society as a whole, they think first and foremost of their own sectional interests. At the very least, therefore, the divisive and adversarial electoral system is another reason why peace is so difficult.

If, however, the democratic process is to be a key part of any peace process, the former must itself be peaceful, and every citizen, when he/she actually participates in the democratic process - i.e., when they vote - should be enabled thereby to perform a personal act of reconciliation. In other words, whenever a highly controversial question is posed, there should always be at least one compromise option on the ballot paper, and preferably, rather more than one. In similar fashion, whenever an election takes place, the Protestant should be able to vote for a Protestant *and* a Catholic, and *vice versa;* Serbs, too, should be able to vote for a Serb *and* a Bosniak *and* a Croat, if they so wish,[5] and again, *vice versa,* twice over.

---

3   See, for example, Woodward, p 212.

4   Newfoundland, for example had a three-option vote, in 1948. The first multi-option referendum was held in Australia in 1920 on what some might consider to be the most controversial question to face any democracy: prohibition. Is it fair to surmise that the necessity of a compromise was therefore paramount? No wonder they opted for a pluralist democracy!
     Just to put all of this into perspective, we should also recall that the first recorded use of a multi-option (plurality) vote took place 1900 years ago, when a certain Pliny the Younger suggested the human being is actually capable of thinking of more than just two opposites. (See Emerson, 1998.)

5   The count, too, must acknowledge the word 'and'. In NI's PR-STV, the single transferable vote is often, as the name suggests, *transferred,* and the vote may go to a Protestant *or* a Catholic; (see p 35). In a Borda system, some points would go to the Serb, *and* others to the Bosniak, *and* again some to the Croat, if indeed such was the voter's stated desire.

The promotion of such democratic structures is this book's second goal, and yet again, it is surprising to see how so few authors actually question the relevant electoral system. Some of them complain about the 'first-past-the-post' method, as we shall see; but very few criticise the obvious defects of PR-List systems; and hardly any propose that which would be more likely to facilitate the election of such persons as would be more able to prevent a war.[6] Accordingly, this book attempts to analyse not only the decision-making processes, (Chapter 5), but also the electoral systems used in the two conflict zones, (Chapter 4). In so doing, it aims to fill what is a huge gap in the study of conflict resolution.

---

6   Even such specialist works as IDEA's *Democracy and Deep-rooted Conflicts; Options for Negotiators* does not discuss the principles upon which a *peaceful* electoral system should be based.

CHAPTER 2

THE SIMILARITIES

"Oh don't worry, we know how to handle this; we were based in Northern Ireland."

A British soldier, a member of the Parachute Regiment, patrolling the streets of Priština, July 1999.

The bloody Irish, they're always fighting. Such statements were often heard, not least from English politicians who thus sought to wash their hands of their own responsibilities in the Northern Ireland conflict.

The bloody Balkans, they're always fighting. *"Ancient hatreds"* was John Major's phrase.[1] The purpose, again, was to reject any thought that the West itself might be partly responsible.

(And talking of things bloody, we should also recall the bloody jokes. The English have been cracking jokes at the expense of the Irish for years and, I'm afraid, a similar scene occurs in the Balkans: 'these' joke about 'those', 'those' about 'the others', and sadly, the ones who come out at the bottom of the pile are the Albanians and, as always, the Roma.)

* * * * * * * *

Those are two, perhaps somewhat glib similarities between the two conflicts. In the paragraphs to come, I'll try to identify a number of other parallels under the following headings, most of which touch on a common theme: our natural inclination to think of most problems in terms of only two variants, and these in turn are incorrectly regarded as mutually exclusive;

Church/state relationships.
Majoritarianism.
The bloody arguments.
Patriarchy.
Academics...
... and politicians.
Journalists.
External factors, and
Any solutions.

* * * * * * *

---

1   Hansard, 23.6.93, quoted in Malcolm ,1996, p xx.

CHURCH/STATE RELATIONSHIPS

An obvious factor in both conflicts is the ghastly mix up there has been, over the years, between religion and nationalism. Is the conflict in Northern Ireland between Catholics and Protestants and/or nationalists and unionists? Is the problem in the former Yugoslavia between Catholics and Orthodox, and Christians and Moslems, and/or between Croats and Serbs and Bosniaks and Albanians? Thirdly, is it not wrong for the churches and the mosque to be so closely identified with one particular political sect?

The answer to the last question, of course, is yes. There were many historical reasons why temporal power became closely associated with the powers spiritual, and we can't change those, of course. The sadness is that those links, even in this so-called sophisticated age, remain. The Catholic church in Ireland considers itself to be Irish; some Protestant denominations, on the other hand, fly the British flag and/or those regimental colours either outside and/or inside the church, and thus make their links equally clear.

Sometimes, of course, there are inter-church contacts, which in theory are good. At the same time, however, there are the greater forces of division, not least the separate schools. That the Protestant and Catholic churches should both wish to have their own schools is perhaps understandable. That the British government should actually fund such segregation is quite inexcusable.

(That it should promote further division in England, with separate schools for Catholics, Protestants, Jews and now Moslems, with maybe others yet to follow, is not only unwise but untenable.) At least Yugoslavia, as a direct benefit of the communist regime, was blessed with a form of integrated, or rather secular, education. Sadly, those days are gone, and 'segregated calculus' is once more back on the syllabus.

So some inter-church contacts are actually harmful to society, as when the two opposites come together because of this shared dislike of integrated education. These and similar forms of co-operation tend to promote, or at least maintain, the division in our society. Like certain peace groups such as *"The Two Traditions"*, both Churches support each other and, in so doing, seek to exclude any "others". In this regard, as we shall see, they resemble those political parties which, in theory, oppose each other, and yet, in practice, actually co-operate in order to maintain that mutual opposition.

In the Balkans, too, various religions are closely associated with so-called national groups. The 'Croat' is the southern Slav who is Catholic. The 'Serb' is the Orthodox southern Slav. Both regard the Bosniak as a converted Croat/ Serb, arguing that 'Moslem' is not a nationality but a religion. It is a criticism which could just as easily be levelled against themselves and their own labels.

The NI Protestant also claims to have an identity, yet that phrase, 'Protestant identity', is actually a contradiction in terms: the adjective refers to that which, by both definition and claim, could be a *universal* phenomenon, while the noun applies to what would be a regional or, at most, a national criterion.

The difference between the Protestant of Ulster and the Catholic/Orthodox of Yugoslavia is this: the former have lost but, by historical accident, the latter have actually won their propaganda war. Both Serbs and Croats have convinced not only themselves but also the rest of the world that they *do* have an identity. Actually, they don't. The only difference between the first- and the second-named Slav is the religious one... plus a thousand years of history, of course, which does make a bit of a difference. But there is no ethnic conflict in what was Yugoslavia, save perhaps in Kosova between the Slavs and the Albanians. Furthermore, as is well known, they all drink the same (Turkish) coffee, love the same good *šlivovic*, enjoy (what to me is) the same good music, share the same sad history... and smoke the same lousy cigarettes. Virtually the only differences were, and are, religious.

Having won that propaganda war, these Serbs and Croats then do what similar groups do, working together to eliminate any "others". This is apparent, first of all, in that attitude of superiority which both Serbs and Croats have towards the Moslems in Bosnia and the Sandžak, and this is then duplicated in their attitude towards yet others in these lands: the Vlahs, for example, the Albanians, the Roma we mentioned, the Macedonians (and the Jews).[2] Northern Ireland also tends to be more racist than other UK societies for, needless to say, religious sectarianism also promotes other forms of bigotry.

Returning to matters ecclesiastical, we should also mention those events which promote individual churches and thus further division in society. The Pope's visit to Ireland should have included the North. After all, he who claims to have the best insurance policy of all should not then use 'security' as an excuse for not crossing an artificial border. Meanwhile, in the Balkans, he has managed to visit Croatia twice, Bosnia once, and Serbia not at all. What's more, he has beatified Cardinal Stepinac, a controversial figure to put it mildly.[3]

On the Protestant front, the established Church of England still maintains the most ancient church-state relationship this side of Belgrade. Heirs to the English throne must declare themselves to be *"good and faithful Protestants"*,[4] that is, anything but a papist! Prime Ministers appoint bishops; bishops then sit in parliament; it is all very much removed from the bible, and it ill-befits a nation which claims to be pluralist, in the best, 'multi-multi' sense of that word. Hopefully, with reform of the House of Lords and so on very much on the current British government's agenda, all that is now changing.

---

2   The Jews, of course, sometimes make the same mistake as the Serbs and the Croats, forgetting that 'religion' is one thing and 'nation' is another. It should be possible for a Jewish Bosnian to be exactly that, but most regard themselves as Bosnian Jews, i.e., Jews who just happen to be in Bosnia.

3   Stepinac was the Catholic cardinal in Zagreb during the second world war, when Croatia was a puppet fascist state under Pavelić or rather, under Hitler; to many, it seemed as if the Catholic Church in Croatia supported this *ustaša* regime.

4   Para 354 of Halsbury's Ecclesiastical Laws of England. Unfortunately, these and other related matters were not discussed in the Belfast Talks, because only the Republic was put 'in the dock', for Articles 2 and 3, and so on. England/Britain/UK, it seems, is innocent!

Some in Northern Ireland go even further, of course, seeking as they do *"a Protestant state for a Protestant people"*. That, however, is either another contradiction in terms, and/or a form of fascism.

The link between church and state in the Balkans is, if anything, stronger. The Catholic churches fly the Croatian flag[5] as proudly as does any Protestant spire on the 12th. And in Serbia, as in England, the Orthodox Church is not only identified with, but named after, the state. Admittedly, it is still part of the Orthodox family, with relations in Greece and Russia etc., but that church/state linkage is still potent, and has been used to effect in the recent wars.[6]

MAJORITARIANISM

We are into politics, and the next similarity between the two conflicts is the fact that nearly all combatants in both conflicts believe in majority rule. Northern Ireland was concocted in order to produce a Protestant majority. And once that majority was in place, it then ruled. That, after all, is democracy, they say.[7]

Well, if Ireland can opt out of the United Kingdom, as it did, then surely Croatia can opt out of Yugoslavia. And if then Northern Ireland can opt out of Ireland, as it did, then surely the *krajina*[8] can opt out of Croatia. Well, no it can't, apparently.

To put it another way, let us think in terms of 1990, or perhaps of 1980, when Tito died. If you have a big box called Yugoslavia, and if you take a majority vote on whether or not to keep Yugoslavia as a nation-state, you will probably have a majority in favour, and admittedly, a minority against. If that minority makes its own middle box [in the big box], calls itself Croatia, and has a vote on whether to be a nation-state, it too will probably have a majority in favour and a minority against. If that second minority then makes a tiny box [in the middle box, in the big box], calls itself the *krajina*, and has a vote on whether or not to be whatever, it too will probably have a majority in favour and yet another minority against. And so on, and so on, *ad nauseam*.

The whole process could repeat and repeat itself, like a Russian *matryoshka* doll, with each box giving way to a smaller box, until every individual declares him/herself to be an independent nation state... of one person! If taken to its logical conclusion, therefore, majority rule does not work. Yet for reasons unclear, virtually the whole world still believes in it,

---

5   The *'šahovica'*, the flag used by the fascist regime of footnote [3], dates back to the middle ages.

6   An orthodox priest was often seen on the political platform of the Serb Radical Party, SRS, the extreme Serb nationalist party of Šešelj.

7   See, for example, the 1996 *Report of the [Irish] Constitution Review Group*, where learned academics agreed, *"Democracy works on the basis of a decision by the majority."* Op. cit., p 398.

8   Areas in Croatia, in what was the Austro-Hungarian Empire, inhabited by Serbs and ruled directly from Vienna as a bulwark against the Ottoman Empire; (see p 21). In similar fashion, by the way, Georgia opted out of the Soviet Union, and Abhazia opted out of Georgia. That, too, caused a war.

not only when the problem is between two opposing factions, as in Northern Ireland, but even when three sides are involved, as in Bosnia.

In Northern Ireland, it is at least inadvisable to use a simple two-option decision-making process like a referendum because, as in war, it tends to force people to take sides. But in Bosnia, as we shall see, any use of a two-option decision-making process was almost bound to have incorrigible consequences.

It too is the same in war, and just as 'nice' countries like Finland found themselves on the 'wrong' side during WWII - if, that is, it was 'wrong' to fight Stalin - so too any two-option vote will often 'force' people to adopt unwise or even horrible policies, each of which may then become either fact or myth, with often yet further horrific consequences.

* * * * * * * *

It is not just in the theory of national sovereignty that majority voting is so obviously inappropriate, for in fact, majority rule very rarely exists. The trouble is, people *think* it exists. And to make matters worse, ambitious politicians either believe it exists, or refuse to question it because it suits their ambitions.

Take, for example, a political party which believes in majority rule, and which takes its own decisions by majority vote. It is therefore an animal which consists of just two wings... (and no body! no wonder it's always in such a flap!) If, then, it elects a leader - Mrs. Thatcher, for some reason, comes to mind - she will represent the dominant wing of that party... (and to take the analogy further, any creature with such a physical characteristic usually goes round in circles). If the party then goes on to win the majority of seats in an election, she assumes the premiership. She wins, yes, but she represents, at best, only a majority of the majority, and 51% of 51% is just 26%.

To be a real majoritarian, therefore, when as in this example, the process involves two votes, she would need at least 71% of 71% to be sure of a 50%+ majority.

* * * * * * * *

On matters of policy, too, it is invariably true to say that majoritarianism does not work at all well. Firstly, there are very few issues which are a question of either 'this' or 'that'. There are, after all, more than two ways of running the economy, more than two educational systems, more than two planning proposals, more than two types of constitutional arrangement, and so on.

Only one question is definitely either/or, 'this' or 'that': which side of the road do we use? A few others, such as whether or not we should join something which already exists, like the European Common Market as the EU used to be called, might possibly be either/or. Pretty well everything else, however, should be a question not just of black or white, but of various shades of grey as well.

Secondly, given our propensity towards majority voting, people invariably pose a two-option question: are you British or Irish? Serb or Croat? Hutu or

Tutsi? they ask (or imply) in national referenda. But on other matters too, in national polls or parliamentary votes, they ask such questions as:

'poll-tax-yes-or-no?'

whereas it should be

'poll-tax-or-local-income-tax-or-property-tax-or-land-tax-or-whatever?'

depending on the debate. Pluralism, after all, should consist of more than just two 'opposites'.

The reason why most democracies do not offer a choice of three or more options is quite simple: in a multi-option vote, politicians would be less able to control the agenda. As we said earlier, opposites don't like "others"; therefore, they try to restrict the debate to a choice of just two options. If, furthermore, you have a majority of seats in parliament, you can then have a debate on poll tax or anything else for that matter, and pretend that this is democracy at work; come the vote, however, you win, always. Parliament is a nonsense.

In a nutshell, majority voting is a means by which politicians (and many committee chairpersons) control the agenda; in most instances, that is all it is; and only in the case of a hung parliament (or a truly humble chair) do leaders forgo their monopoly control.

* * * * * * * *

We cannot blame just the few unionist and nationalist politicians, who have both sought to dominate their opposites for so many years; nor should we heap our disapproval on those Bosnian, Croat and Serb 'leaders' who argue and fight to gain a majority. For sadly, virtually the whole world believes in what is nevertheless a myth!

The disadvantages of such simplistic thinking are many, and one in particular should be recalled, log-rolling,[9] and it works like this. Associations and parliaments, even in undivided societies, are often split down the middle. This is especially true of any two-party, Anglo-Saxon parliamentary system such as exists in the UK or USA. Therefore, in any two-option vote, it will be the few folks in the middle, the floating voters, who will make all the difference. And maybe they float because for one reason or another, they are not particularly interested in the matter under debate.

So if, for example, you are concerned about nuclear power and I'm obsessed with dog-licences, you can persuade me to vote with you, and *vice versa*. With such thinking, the unionists were bought by successive governments in London to vote in parliament on matters totally unrelated to the union, yet for the sake of that union. The vote on Maastricht was a case in point. In similar fashion, and here any of us who are UK tax-payers must hang our heads in shame, John

---

9   An American term. I am not trying to say that multi-option voting will eliminate such wheeling and dealing; as long as all parliamentary votes are in the public domain, however, such tactics will be much more difficult to conceal.

Major decided to support Germany's bid for early recognition of Croatia, for the sake of his petty little opt-out clause on the social chapter![10]

* * * * * * * *

Majority voting, then, does not work well, even at the best of times and in the most peaceful of societies. In lands divided by religion or whatever, it does not and cannot work at all; Kosova proves that! If NATO wants Kosovo to be the home of both Serbs and Albanians, there is absolutely no point whatsoever in using a majority vote in that province! In other conflicts, also, although perhaps it is not so graphically obvious, majority voting is part of the problem. It was not just the abuses but also the uses of majority rule which led to the NI troubles. And in the Balkans, it was the very change-over from communism to majoritarianism which caused most to argue and many to fight. To quote just one simple example: *"The Croatian people in Bosnia and Herzegovina cannot agree... because they know that they as a minority would be subject to majority rule..."*[11]

The fault lies, however, not only with those who practice majoritarianism to the exclusion of other ethnic groups, but also with those who, in non-conflict societies, use exactly the same techniques in pursuit of their own ambitions. Both Blair and Ahern now recognise that majority rule does not work in Belfast, yet neither have considered using a more inclusive methodology in their own parliaments. It is with exactly the same hypocrisy that the international community tells the Balkan peoples that they too must be 'democratic'.

THE BLOODY ARGUMENTS

As soon as the people have divided, if not indeed before, you hear the reasons why such divisions were so necessary. And the arguments in Northern Ireland are often the same as those heard in the Balkans. Here are a few of them.

* * * * * * * *

This is our land, they say, as if land can actually belong to anybody! And is this your snow? I asked one Bosnian Croat. Unfortunately, in western European civilisation, people believe that you *can* own *"the freshness of the air, or the sparkle of the water"*.[12] And having acquired some land by means fair or foul, they then build fences, take out insurance policies and deploy armed forces, all to defend *"the rights of property"*.

Now as it so happens, the Celtic peoples came from somewhere in the Balkans. If, therefore, the theory were sound, Ireland would not belong to the

---

10   See Woodward, p 184.

11   President Tudjman, contradicting himself as usual, at a press conference in April 1992. He used and wildly abused majority rule in Croatia against the *krajina* Serbs, but could not accept the logic for any Croats elsewhere. He was not the only one to make that mistake, of course. Quoted in Silber and Little, p 325.

12   To quote Chief Seattle's testimony.

Irish, and nor would Serbia belong to the Serbs. Instead, Serbia would be part of the Irish Empire, and maybe the Serbs would be back in Slovakia, or somewhere near the Caspian Sea, where they came from many years ago, before borders were invented.

* * * * * * * *

We have our culture, they also say. That's even more problematic. For while some Protestants march up and down various highways playing ancient Irish melodies,[13] other Protestants in other lands do no such thing! Or look at the Balkan problem: the Croats were Croats and the Serbs were Serbs, long before they were Christian, yet ask either about culture, and all you get is a diatribe about churches, monasteries, and ancient religious rituals. In fact, as often as not, that's what you get even when you don't ask for it!

* * * * * * * *

We were here first, they say, the Protestants only came a few hundred years ago. Folks, therefore, are again divided into two: the indigenous and the settlers. If, however, the fact that the Protestants did come from somewhere else removes some right or other - Americans beware - the fact that the Celts also came from somewhere should remove their right as well.

When 'here' is the Balkans, or part of the Balkans, the Albanians were here first. Well, they think they were first, claiming as they do to be descended from the Illyrians. There again, there were a few other folks around, not least those Vlahs again, who surely would have equal rights if there was anything right at all. The Slavs, everyone agrees, came later, in about the sixth century AD, although other Slavs came a little earlier via a different route, to Bulgaria and Macedonia. Given, however, that the tides of history have ebbed and flowed, that peoples have fought and loved, have occupied and fled, have converted and migrated and sometimes been assimilated, to talk of someone being either 'this' or 'that' is often inaccurate.

* * * * * * * *

If they've lost some of the above arguments, they might then say, this is our native tongue. And if it isn't, they'll pretend it is. Some Protestants, for example - and even some Gaelic speakers! - have decided that Ulster Scots is a language. In similar fashion, the head of broadcasting in Zagreb, having first told me that his fifteen years in Australia had given him an open mind, then tried to say that Croatian was totally different from Serbian. And there I was, clutching my *'Teach-yourself-Serbo-Croat'*.

Having convinced themselves of a nonsense, they then argue for all sorts of cultural rights such as separate schools. It's back to religion again. By this time, however, the arguments are beginning to turn personal. It came as no surprise, but it was still sad to hear both in Belfast and in the Balkans, 'these'

---

13 *'The Sash'* was originally a lament on the sectarian divisions in our society, a Scots-Irish love song called *'Irish Mollyo'*.

complain that 'those' are dirty, or 'those' that 'these' have too many children. In similar fashion, I often heard 'them' complain that the other 'they' had committed such-and-such an atrocity during such-and-such a political event, during such-and-such an historical occasion, during such-and-such a century... and so it goes on and on, backwards. In many instances, some of these accusations of course were true; in some instances, though, they were gross exaggerations if not complete fabrications. And it was always 'them' and 'us'.

PATRIARCHY

By now, however, each side has decided that they are, in fact, quite different from their supposed opposites. They have different churches to confirm that difference, and different schools to perpetuate it. All they need now are different political institutions to confirm those differences, and none to confirm any similarities, (none such as a 'British-Irish Council ' which we are soon, at last, to have here, or a Balkan Federation which is still only on the agenda over there). But first, before we tackle the politics, there is one other sociological factor needed to perpetuate these supposed differences.

If you meet someone called Sammy Thompson, he may just be a Protestant. Marie Kelly, on the other hand, might possibly be a Catholic. Similarly, in Yugoslavia, the name often tells the sectarian everything he needs to know. There are exceptions in both places, but it still works as a pretty good indicator.

Such a fool-proof system is protected by one very simple tradition: the patriarchal society. With all those tides of history we referred to, there is a strong possibility that the great-great-great-grandchild will not be of the same 'ethnic' stock as the very great (mum and) dad. It was therefore decided that the child shall have daddy's surname, and daddy's nominal religion, and who mummy was shall be of no concern at all. How else could society be divided so 'neatly' into only two in Northern Ireland and Croatia, or just three in Bosnia?

It is easy to see how, in a supposedly ethnic conflict, such a misguided logic could lead some to the crime of rape. There is, nevertheless, no such thing as an ethnically pure 'people'. Furthermore, if there were such folk, they would probably be the result of such an incestuous parentage as to be all quite mad... which may explain quite a lot.

ACADEMICS

There are, then, obvious inaccuracies in calling someone either British or Irish, either Serb or Croat, and so on, yet it is amazing just how many people actually do do this. Statisticians, journalists, political researchers, social scientists and even peace activists insist on drawing these orange and green maps of Belfast which might represent something, or those multi-coloured portraits of Bosnia which tend to look like an Irish stew, each pretending we are what we most definitely are not, that we are 'this' or 'that' but seldom 'other'! In so doing, I fear, if but to small effect, they are actually perpetuating the problem.

Those who write our history books also fall into this trap, for some have written different variations of that which, after all, was only one theme. Now in many ways, Ireland has been quite lucky. We have a tiny history, if but because we are stuck on the edge of the Euro-Asian landmass, and apart from the odd Roman and a couple of Vikings, there was only one empire to worry about. Even so, there have always been at least two interpretations of what then followed. In the Balkans, however, in this century alone, they have had the Austro-Hungarians, the Ottomans, the Russians, the British, the Italians and the Germans, amongst others. The potential for differences in emphasis and interpretation is therefore huge.

Despite the above, both intellectuals and journalists in Northern Ireland try to make our simple history complicated. It is easily done. Human tales are full of details. But maybe part of our problem is this pretence that it is so complex, and not least because complexity itself then allows for different interpretations.

But let's look at a complicated story. At the beginning of the nineteenth century, with the British Empire coming into its apogee, the Ottoman Empire started to decline. After four hundred years of imperial diktat, some of the Slav peoples at last had the chance to assert their own place among what we euphemistically call the family of nations.

Croatia, of course, was still a colony of the Austro-Hungarian Empire and, until the revolutions of 1848, the latter showed fewer signs of senility. Not yet, therefore, could Zagreb seek its independence. If anything was to happen, it would come from inside Istanbul's remit, in one or other of those lands which to-day we call Albania, Bosnia, Bulgaria, Greece, Macedonia, Montenegro, Romania or Serbia. Given, however, that Serbia was at the periphery of this Turkish empire, it was perhaps inevitable that the first revolts would happen there. They did so, somewhat accidentally as it happened, in 1804.

That was the time to fight, and that was the time to write, or re-write, the history books. The nineteenth century was the dawn of nationalism, and each group of people described their own histories in the most glorious terms. In the reign of Tsar Dušan in the 14th century, Serbia included all of Kosovo and extended way down into present day Albania and Greece; that was their glorious epoch. Under King Tvrtko in 1391, Bosnia stretched from the rivers Drina and Sava in the east and north, to a broad stretch of the Adriatic in the south-west. Croatia also claims a magnificence from when a certain Tomislav declared himself to be king, in the year 924. Each people remembers their hey-day. And each has its intellectual historians to make it all sound true.

Sadly, the process continues to this day. The rise of Milošević was based largely on the work of certain intellectuals in Belgrade, for in 1987 they produced some wild xenophobic exaggerations which they nevertheless called facts. It is not just the historians, of course, who make these intellectual errors, creating artificial divisions between peoples. As mentioned earlier, we are all prone to this mistake, when we participate in the 'black-or-white' rituals of majoritarianism.

... AND POLITICIANS

"History," E P Thompson once said, is *"a succession of blunders"*. This is partly because those who make decisions are often, first and foremost, politicians more interested in the pursuit of power and less concerned about humanity. And this, in turn, is in large measure the consequence of a political culture which actually makes it more likely that such people will become our 'leaders'.

Take, for example, the Belfast peace talks which, in one guise or another, went on for years; or take the Geneva peace talks on the Bosnian crisis; both involved maybe some of the right people, but some of the wrong people too. To take the extreme example, did Karadžić (and at a later stage, Milošević) have to represent *all* the Bosnian Serbs?

Furthermore, in both conflicts, most of the participants in the peace process were, to put it at its least emphatic, the very people who had failed to prevent the violence. Sometimes, and definitely in the case of Karadžić, they were the antagonists who had caused the bloody mayhem. Why, then, were they (and only they) the representatives of their (sic) people (sic)? Is this, again, because the world believes in majoritarianism?

We will discuss that which goes by the name of diplomacy when we analyse the crisis in Kosova. Suffice to say at this stage that because those outsiders who guide the peace processes are themselves politicians, and majoritarian politicians to boot, there is an overriding tendency for them to remain within current political thinking. Both in Belfast and in Bosnia, international mediators believe the democratic process must be an intrinsic part of the peace process. In theory, they are right.

But in practice, in its present *modus operandi*, the democratic process is not itself 'peace-ful'. It starts, at the very beginning, when the ambitious nominate themselves to stand as candidates. Vote for me, they plead, in a process which cannot enhance their modesty. Furthermore, to gain election, they join forces with others in political parties, literally to fight (electorally) other political parties.

There are already two weaknesses in the system. Firstly, the candidate has at least two loyalties, one to his party, and the other to his electorate, (let alone a third to himself). If ever there is to be a clash between the two, he will undoubtedly obey his party's bidding - the appropriately-called *whip* system - for if he loses the party whip, he will undoubtedly lose his seat.

Secondly, the very electoral system - be it majoritarian (plurality) or, to a lesser extent, a form of proportional representation - actually encourages each party to compete against some or even all of the others. He who gets the largest minority or the PR quota gets elected. All he needs is his faction, and his chances of getting their support may actually be enhanced by antagonising the opposition. His obligation, therefore, is only to his party and/or those who elected him. It is not to society as a whole.

Why, then, is such a 'representative' a delegate in a peace process? Is he trying to secure a peace for everyone? Or is he there to get the most for his own sectional interest?

There is another factor here, of course, for why is it that the democratic process - the very instrument by which, in theory, society is able to progress - nevertheless elects the same old faces? The answer lies in part with those other would-be members of the intelligentsia, the journalists. In theory, in any election, every candidate is on an equal footing, both old and new alike. In practice, however, an industry increasingly oriented to over-simplification often decides that there are, in fact, just a few favourites. Inevitably, these are the old faces. Therefore they get coverage. Therefore they win. The new, in effect, are in a catch 22.

In Northern Ireland in any pre-election campaign, the media will act in this way, basing any coverage of events not so much on what is said, more on who has said it, and this they do because of the Representation of the People's Act, a pretence at fairness designed by the big parties to perpetuate their bigness. In Bosnia, such a bias has not been legislated for, not yet anyway, but the effect is the same because wittingly or unwittingly, the international community gives more emphasis to those particular old faces, who, as it were by definition, still believe in the past.

JOURNALISTS

This brings us to another similarity between the two conflicts: the role of the media. In Belfast, you'll find them in the Europa Hotel. In Bosnia, they were staying in the Holiday Inn, the ugliest building in Sarajevo we mentioned in the introduction. In Priština, they are ensconced in The Grand Hotel. And in each conflict zone, the 'hack pack' as they now call themselves exchange stories. If one gets it wrong, they might all make the same mistake.[14]

Given their background which is usually of a western European orientation, they often go with that sort of tide. Furthermore, they sometimes tend to follow the politics of the 'international community'.

---

14 It was the same in Bucharest, where they stayed in the Intercontinental; and the same again in Moscow where, by order of the state, they were forced to live together in special compounds. So, inevitably, they sometimes tended to write the same sort of stories. In 1990, I tried to persuade the Irish Times correspondent that Boris Yeltsin was no good; unfortunately, however, he (Conor O'Cleary) and many others decided that Boris was only brilliant; and the internal effects of such external approval were not inconsiderable.

When the time came to demonise the Serbs, for example, they did so with relish; there again, with the fall of Vukovar and the rape camps in Bosnia, there was much good reason. Nevertheless, it was wrong to vilify *all* Serbs. It was equally wrong to praise *all* Croats, Bosnians and/or Kosovar Albanians.

EXTERNAL FACTORS

As we saw in the re-writing of history books, countries tend to remember their most glorious period. Serbia aspires to a Greater Serbia. Croatia does likewise. Albania is also guilty. But no country is Great, unless of course we are all great. Accordingly, and in the interests of both Northern Ireland and the Balkans, the only other country to use such an adjective should cease to do so and call itself just Britain.

* * * * * * * *

In Northern Ireland, people aspired to centres of power which were beyond its borders, and those two centres - London and Dublin - were long in open conflict, each insisting we were all either/or. In Bosnia, the picture was as always a little more complicated: many Catholic Bosnians aspired to Zagreb, most Orthodox Bosnians[15] to Belgrade, and only the progressive along with the mainly Moslem population gave their allegiance to their own republic/country.

With the signing of the Anglo-Irish Agreement in 1985, the British and Irish governments came, at last, to a meeting of minds. That was the start of the Peace Process. In Bosnia, both Milošević and Tudjman, one indicted and one suspected war criminal, were involved in the Dayton peace accords, but not yet, I fear, are either Belgrade or Zagreb committed to a Bosnian future.

* * * * * * * *

As with the British Empire in Northern Ireland, so too with many imperial powers in the Balkans, the role of the external powers has always been a considerable factor. Indeed, as we will see in the next chapter, external forces were *always* embroiled in what has been described as the 'cockpit of history'. In earlier times, they were 'protecting' 'their' vested interests. To-day, some of them are still at that work, while others are less consciously promoting western beliefs - freedom, a free press, free elections, a free market, but first and foremost, the free movement of capital (which is the end of freedom, of course).

Throughout the years of the Cold War, both Northern Ireland and Yugoslavia were regarded as important. (There again, to the military mind, even an uninhabited island may have strategic significance.) For years, Reagan and company were trying to persuade the Republic of Ireland to join NATO, as a *quid pro quo* for eventual Irish unity.

---

15 Many Catholic and Orthodox Bosnians regard themselves, not as Bosnians of course, but as Croats and Serbs respectively.

And ever since Tito broke with Stalin in 1948, the West supported the Yugoslav Stalinist because of his opposition to the Soviet one. But more of all that in the next chapter. Suffice here to point out that the above Anglo-Irish Agreement was signed the year Gorbachev came to power and the year, therefore, in which Northern Ireland lost any strategic importance.

At the same time, of course, Yugoslavia lost her strategic importance as well. The West maintained a financial interest only, for Belgrade was in debt.[16]

* * * * * * * *

A further contrast concerns the whole question of international intervention and peace-keeping. In 1969, in Northern Ireland, the local situation was definitely out of hand, and an outside, impartial presence was essential. They sent in the British army. It was at least a pity that that chosen force was not international in nature.

Part of the problem, of course, was the fact that Britain, a world and UN-veto power, was party to the conflict; the UK was hardly going to agree to any outside 'interference' into what it argued was its own 'internal affair', even though it has now agreed that Ireland also has an interest.

In 1999, in contrast, NATO went into Kosova on the pretext that the local administration was infringing the Kosovars' human rights (to put it mildly), and despite the fact that Serbia regarded Kosova as its own internal concern.

Although many years have since passed, let us nevertheless consider what is now only a hypothetical question. But *IF* the intervening force in Northern Ireland in 1969 had been international, it might well have included personnel from some neutral countries, and in particular some persons from the non-aligned nations.[17] In other words, some Yugoslavs might have been patrolling the streets of Belfast, running our prisons and/or helping to administer our courts.

If such had been the case, I am sure the overall casualty figures for the thirty years of the troubles would have been less. But more than that, of course. It might also have helped the Yugoslavs to prevent, or at least gain a warning of, their own wars of the 1990s.

It remains an 'if' of history.

ANY SOLUTIONS

If there are similarities in the problems, there must, of course, be parallels in the resolutions of these conflicts. And yes, there are a number.

---

16 See fn 8 on p 25.

17 The first meeting of 'The Conference of Non-aligned Nations' was held in Belgrade in September 1961, when Tito was host to 25 heads of state from all over the world.

Firstly, it is always good to have some form of arbitration, and such should best be impartial. Even in Northern Ireland, then, although the intervening power was the partial British and is now both the partial British and the partial Irish, it was nevertheless felt sensible to invite such as the American, Senator George Mitchell, to chair the talks, along with a few others from Canada and Finland to look after de-commissioning.

In Bosnia and Kosova, the international community is, at least in theory, impartial. If it was the UN and not NATO, and if the UN (and OSCE) were properly structured so as to be independent of national interests, it could be even more impartial.

Secondly, societies which have become divided need such political institutions as ensure none feel alienated - in most instances, these are made manifest in those political chambers which confirm their various differences: not just one parliament in London, but an independent one in Dublin as well; not just one centralised power in Belgrade, but separate and equal administrations in Ljubljana, Zagreb, Sarajevo and so on.

As implied on p 13, however, it is quite wrong and very dangerous not to have such other institutions as will confirm any similarities. It has taken a long time to get a British-Irish Council in these islands,[18] even though the Scandinavian countries have long since set the example in the form of their Nordic Union. And despite many proposals, there is yet to be a Balkan Federation. The EU may eventually provide some cohesion, but it lacks a certain intimacy! So given recent history, in addition to any separate centres of power, there must also be that common political institution which can reflect if only the common history these unlucky people share.

In fact, of course, Yugoslavia was a brave attempt at creating just such a federal unit, even if it did only relate to part of the Balkans, and not even to all the 'Southern Slavs', namely, those in Bulgaria. How unfortunate it is that so many refer to this in the past, by using the term *"the former Yugoslavia"*. Or am I being too optimistic when I use two adjectives: *"the former and future Yugoslavia"*?

* * * * * * * *

Thirdly and finally, any solution to either conflict must include more inclusive democratic structures, both in any electoral systems, and in any decision-making processes, be they parliamentary, national or international. Of which, of course, more anon.

---

18 Sadly, the two governments still insist, now in the peace, just as they did throughout the 'war', that we mere citizens can only be either/or. This divisiveness is now enshrined in the Good Friday Agreement, (see p 46).

CHAPTER 3

WAR AND THE THEORY OF WAR

"The French will only be united under the threat of danger.
No-one can simply bring together a country that has 265 kinds of cheese."

Charles de Gaulle
President of France, speaking in 1951.[1]

Bosnia, 1993, war, and somewhere to the north-east of Sarajevo, a little boy was playing in the woods, and he got lost. The soldiers who found him asked him his name. Feljko Tapić, he replied, and they immediately realised what had happened. He was now in enemy territory, and he just hadn't understood the madness of this adult world, that a battle had raged, and that the occupied territories had been re-defined. The soldiers took him to the freshly dug trenches, the new front line.

Gospodin Tapić, (Mr. Tapić), they shouted across to the woods beyond. Silence.

GOSPODIN TAPIĆ, they yelled. Again, nothing moved.

GOSPODIN TAPIĆ, they repeated, WE HAVE YOUR SON! There was a pause, and then, at last, a reply from someone unseen: let him speak. So the soldiers brought the boy forward, and he said in his little eight-year old voice: *Papa, ja sam.* (It's me, daddy.)

Both sides now knew the case was genuine. A cease-fire was arranged, the guns were put down, unarmed soldiers stood up, and the young fellow was re-united with his father. They went home. With what there was in the larder, mum baked a few little cakes. But before the young lad ate any, he and his dad went back to the front line, another cease-fire was arranged, and he took some buns across to the enemy.[2]

* * * * * * * *

The history of the Anglo-Irish conflict has been described in many volumes elsewhere, and there are only two points I wish to make here, which relates to the very nature of conflict, the fact that *"your neighbour is your enemy".*

---

1 A quotation taken from *In a Dark Time*, edited by Nicholas Humphrey and Robert Jay Lipton, Faber and Faber, 1984, p 53.

2 A story related to the author by one of the Bosnian refugees then living in Dublin. The names used are quite fictitious, but the facts are by no means unique.

Initially, the various dukes in Ireland were fighting each other, as neighbouring dukes used to do. When one started to lose, he sought help from the English, who came, saw, conquered, and just forgot to leave.[3]

In the years which followed the revolution in Paris in 1789, London was worried that the French would attack England via the back-door, Ireland. After all, ever since the dukes had stopped fighting dukes and countries had started to fight countries, England and France had been enemies. Eventually, of course, they became friends, but only when the world entered another era, as countries formed alliances, and whole blocs fought each other, as in the two world wars.

In 1798, however, given not only that, *"your neighbour is your enemy,"* but also *"your neighbour's neighbour is your friend"*, Ireland and France were allies, united by a common foe, the English, and a French force landed in Ireland in support of an Irish uprising. They lost.

By 1978, the enemy had changed, but the thinking was exactly the same. Britain now feared an attack by Soviet 'bear' aircraft flying from the Kola peninsula around the top of Norway and down into the Atlantic, there to set off their cruise missiles, somewhere over (Northern) Ireland. For that reason, the province had a strategic importance throughout the era of the Cold War, and it was only with the advent of Mikhail Gorbachev and his policy of *'perestroika'* that there came an end to its strategic role. Hence, as we mentioned on p 18, the Anglo-Irish Agreement.

* * * * * * * *

The story in the Balkans was different of course, but the same laws of history apply. It too has been recorded elsewhere, and there now follows just a brief description of the three tragedies to afflict that peninsula in the twentieth century: World War I, World War II, and the end of the Cold War. In a word, I will attempt to explain what many consider to be the inexplicable behaviour of the combatants in Yugoslavia, those people who, they say, are always bloody fighting.

Let's first go back a few centuries, to the years when Austria and Turkey were neighbours, and when wars between the two were not infrequent. Anyone who helped to weaken the other was an automatic friend, of course, so the Austrians and the Serbs came to an agreement. The latter settled along the border areas - in the *krajina* we mentioned, (p 8) - and acted as frontiersmen. In the nineteenth century, however, Serbia and others began to (write new history books and) claim their national status. Relationships were bound to be affected.

---

3   The Irish King of Leinster, Dermot Macmurragh, invited the Earl of Pembroke (Strongbow) to help him, which Strongbow did with enthusiasm, first by joining him in battle, then by marrying his daughter, and finally, by succeeding to his throne. Such success should not be allowed to go to the head, thought the King of England, Henry II, who then invaded Ireland, not so much to conquer the Irish, more to subdue the now mighty Earl.

Indeed, by 1878, the Balkans were changing quite rapidly. Bulgaria had just fought a war against the Ottomans, with another of Turkey's neighbours, Russia, joining in as well, supposedly on behalf of her Slav and Orthodox kin. Borders were being re-drawn, ambitions were getting out of hand, and everything had to be settled. Accordingly, the international community (though not then so named) met in the Congress of Berlin to sort it all out. Bulgaria was told to be smaller, Serbia's new borders (which did not then include Kosovo) were recognised, and Bosnia-Herzegovina was given to Austria... much to the annoyance of the Serbs. (Having 'sorted out' the Balkans, the European powers returned to Berlin a couple of years later, to draw all those other borders in Africa; phew, being an imperial ruler was very hard work!)

In a changing world, static agreements sometimes don't work. Trends continue, pressures build up, and then they burst. The Ottoman Empire weakened further. Various ambitions in Belgrade, Sofia, Podgorica, Tirana and Athens, under the ever anxious eyes of Zagreb, were sometimes at one but often at variance, if not indeed totally mutually exclusive. Nevertheless, in 1912, the little (Christian) dogs of the Balkans declared war on Turkey, and they won. Each gained something: Serbia, for example, liberated or occupied (depending on your point of view) Kosova and Macedonia. But one year later, the little dogs fought amongst themselves over the spoils. Initially it was Bulgaria versus Serbia - so much for Slav brotherhood (and Russian propaganda)! But the other dogs soon joined in as well, as dogs do, and so too did the big dog, Turkey. As has so often been told, it all finished with the assassination of the Archduke Franz Ferdinand in Sarajevo, the bombing of Belgrade as Austria declared war on its new neighbour, and the inevitable escalation by which nearly every neighbour of nearly every other neighbour took sides in what rapidly became World War I.

If anything, it was a European civil war between the two 'Great Powers', England and Germany. Yet fighting raged throughout the Balkans, creating victims in one tragedy and myths for another. Both the super-powers (and many smaller nations) were guilty. It was therefore unwise for London to heap all the blame onto Berlin, as happened at Versailles. The result, we all know, was fascism. A more positive result was the creation of Yugoslavia, or the Kingdom of Serbs, Croats and Slovenes, as it was originally called. (So much for the Bosnians, Macedonians and Montenegrins, although they were at least Slavs; and so much too for the Albanians in Kosova).

* * * * * * * *

By 1938, another war looked inevitable, not in the Balkans but on the scale writ large. Either it would be between Germany and one neighbour, to the west; or it would involve the east, Russia, and in the opinion of both London and Berlin, that most dreaded of all evils, bolshevism. In a weird dance called diplomacy, pairs of the triplet tried to tango, so that only the other two would fight. Hence, in 1938, two of them signed the Munich Agreement; and, as a direct consequence, in 1939, a different pair signed the Molotov/Ribbentrop Pact.

The latter was based on the fact that the two big dogs in question - Russia and Germany - had a common neighbour: Poland. They therefore decided to gobble up this little bitch, a fairly frequent fate for the Poles.[4] From Stalin's point of view, you could say he had no choice. As a result of Munich, Hitler already had a huge empire consisting of Germany, Austria and now Czechoslovakia. Either it would soon contain all of Poland as well; or it would have only half of it. He therefore chose the latter, signed, and in 1939, the two armies marched in. The trouble now, of course, was that the two 'friends', Germany and Russia, became neighbours, and enemies. The rest is history: 1941, operation Barbarossa, and the subsequent deaths of about twenty million Russians, as three sides fought the one war. With the defeat of Hitler and the removal, therefore, of one side, another war started between the erstwhile allies, the Cold War.

1941 also saw the German invasion of the Balkans. The Italians were already in (a greater) Albania, the Nazis took control of Belgrade, and a Croat fascist regime under Pavelić was established in Zagreb to rule both Croatia and Bosnia. There were two resistance movements: the (mainly Serb) *četniks* under Mihailović wanted to re-establish the Yugoslav (Serb) monarchy, while Tito's (Croat, Moslem and some Serb) partisans were the very opposite.

Yet again, therefore, there were three sides in dispute, and the means of resolving that dispute was the two-sided process called war. No wonder there were atrocities, with charges of collaboration and betrayal flowing thick and fast, not least when Churchill chose to support Tito's communists.[5] In the internecine warfare in the Balkans, Yugoslavia lost 1,700,000 dead and was left with 3,500,000 homeless.[6]

After the Red Army beat the Germans at the Battle of Stalingrad, it started to march west, and not only the Poles got worried. Needless to say, the latter did not want to replace the rule of the vile fascist dog by that of the communist canine, most especially if the latter was to be Russia, their neighbour and enemy since the days of Ivan the Terrible! Hence, in 1943, the Warsaw uprising.

In theory, the Poles and the Russians were allies, fighting the common enemy of fascism. In practice, of course, as we all know, just as Churchill had delayed the opening up of the western front while the nazis were fighting the bolsheviks, so too the Russians stood on the banks of the Vistula, while Hitler's troops literally flattened Warsaw. The Soviets did not want to be confronted by a Polish intelligentsia, so they let the Germans kill them in the sewers of the ghetto, just as they themselves had killed the officer corps in the forests of Katyn.[7-PTO]

---

4   The three earlier partitions of Poland took place in 1772, 1793 and 1795, at the hands of Austria, Prussia and Russia.

5   Fitzroy Maclean gives a fascinating account of this story in his biography of Tito.

6   See Singleton, p 206.

At the end of WWII, there was a huge demand to ensure that the mistakes of fascism would never be repeated. The League of Nations had failed on a number of occasions, not least when Italy had invaded Albania and Kosova. The United Nations was not to repeat such errors.

Yet from its very inception, the UN was at fault. It was, after all, designed by three old men: Stalin, Churchill and Roosevelt. Each were imperial leaders, each wanted to maintain their own imperial spheres of influence - the Soviet Union, the British Empire and the Monroe Doctrine respectively - and each supposed ally was deeply suspicious of the other two. Accordingly, the UN was born, yet is not the very title a contradiction in terms, supposedly 'uniting' the very 'nations' which by definition were designed to divide? Little wonder, then, that it is only an international and not a supranational organisation.

Like the monarchs who preceded them, these imperial rulers did not want anyone else to interfere in what they regarded as their internal affairs. Therefore, the Charter of Human Rights said virtually nothing about electoral systems. Every country was to have an election, of course, but the choice of system was not going to be stipulated. The USSR had one system, in which every comrade had a choice of one candidate; the USA and the UK had theirs, wherein everyone had a choice of two. Neither system was particularly good. But none of this triumvirate of world leaders was going to improve matters.

On decision-making, they said even less. Politicians, as we said, like to control things. Internationalism and democracy are all very well, but... The little dogs, therefore, could meet in the General Assembly, and vote for-or-against whatever they wanted. Ultimate power, however, would remain with those who barked the loudest, and the veto was given by those who had the power to give it, to themselves, the five (soon to be) nuclear powers.

* * * * * * * *

We may therefore conclude that the first two Balkan tragedies of this century - in 1912/14 and 1941 - were both the result of external factors: the collapse of one empire, the Ottoman, and the invasion of another, Hitler's Germany. The third tragedy, the break-up of Yugoslavia, was also exacerbated, if not indeed caused, by external events.

Like the NI peace process, it also started in Moscow, in 1985, with the advent of Gorbachev and his policy of 'perestroika'. This was excellent news, of course, and the West decided to support him and his policies, which included the maintenance of the Soviet Union. It was, after all, in our vested interest to do so. Stable borders are good for trade, and an open market meant the West could get all those nice resources from Siberia. (Furthermore, if we persuaded the Russians to initiate certain economic 'reforms', the rouble would float, then it would sink, and all that oil would be even cheaper!)

---

7   In 1943, the Germans discovered these mass graves, not far from Smolensk, where the Soviets had executed thousands of young Polish officers in 1941. The Kremlin only admitted this crime in 1990.

In international diplomacy, it seems, one federation (USSR) is like another (FRY). Accordingly, we supported the maintenance of other borders in Eastern Europe, such as those of Yugoslavia.[8] They are inviolable, we stated, and we signed treaties to that effect. But we also said that peoples have the right to self-determination, and thus we contradicted ourselves. (This subject is an absolute minefield, so we'll go into it in a bit more detail in Chapter 5.)

In 1987, after a nasty nationalist speech in Kosovo, Milošević came to power in a bloodless coup. Never mind, we had signed that paper, we still wanted our Siberian oil, we still wanted to maintain stability and therefore all existing borders, so we supported Milošević and we said so.

Then, however, things started to go wrong. Lots of peoples in the Soviet Union wanted to exercise this so-called right of self-determination and to claim their independence. Gorbachev (and Yeltsin, as we said on p 1) knew this was a quagmire, for if you let one lot go, maybe the others will want to go too, and in a land of 120 different nationalities, from the Estonians in the west to the Chukchis in the east, such a policy could cause mayhem. Furthermore, if Russia lost her Siberian oil fields, she would have an even greater economic disaster than what she already had! Therefore, Gorbachev said no, and he used force to implement that 'no'.

In Lithuania on 13th January 1991, fifteen people were killed. The Soviets had killed some in Georgia and Azerbaijan as well, but Lithuania, we felt, was different. After all, it's in Europe - (well, so are the Caucasus, aren't they?) - what's more, people in the Baltics are white.[9] Therefore, we decided to ditch Gorbachev and back Yeltsin;[10] what a disaster that was! And because 'USSR equals FRY', we chose to ditch Milošević and support Tudjman[11] as well.

* * * * * * * *

By this time, however, everything in the Balkans was getting out of hand. Both Slovenia and Croatia wanted self-determination, both were suing for independence, both held referendums, and both descended into war. The first was a relatively minor skirmish, but the second conflict was ghastly.

---

8   *"... preoccupations with stability in the Soviet Union and the risks of its disintegration... dictated the hope of many that Yugoslavia would remain united."* Woodward, p 164, but she goes on to say that *"In fact, the primary interest in holding Yugoslavia together came from the international banking consortium concerned about debt servicing and re-payment."* Ibid, p 383. There again, maybe it was these bankers who first prompted the subsequent Yugoslavian collapse; (see p 53).

9   On April 9th 1989, Soviet troops killed sixteen demonstrators in Tbilisi; on 20th January of the following year, soldiers forced their way into Baku, killing 93 persons.

10   See footnote on p 16.

11   More than any other external factor, this probably determined the subsequent course of events, giving ultimate victory to Tudjman and eventual humiliation to Milošević. If the West had stuck to the inviolability of borders principle, Yugoslavia (and Milošević) might have survived. Izetbegović once remarked, by the way, that *"choosing between Tudjman and Milošević was like having to choose between leukaemia and a brain tumour"*. Malcolm, 1994, p 228.

Now the politics of a collapsing Yugoslavia were comparable to what had been the situation writ large in Europe of 1938. Croatia and Serbia were neighbours and therefore potential enemies. At the same time, these two republics shared a common border with Bosnia which, as already noted, each regarded as 'theirs'; on this point, therefore, they were allies. Milošević and Tudjman hated each other, of course; but they also hated their mutual "other". Hence the dreadful scene, in 1991, when they went to war in Croatia, while at the same time, they were able to hold secret meetings over the division of Bosnia.[12]

A further parallel between WWII and the Bosnia war relates to the Warsaw up-rising and the siege of Sarajevo. In theory, the Croats could have broken that siege quite easily. But, as I mentioned in the introduction, they were just sitting in Kiseljak, drinking a beer, and watching it all happen. Sarajevo was not one of their war aims. They wanted 'only' Mostar, Herzegovina and other parts of western Bosnia. Therefore, at that stage, they did nothing.[13]

In fact, of course, it was worse than that. In 1992, having first joined with the (mainly Moslem) Bosniaks in a vote for independence, they fought *with* them and *against* the Serbs. One year later, however, they fought *against* the Moslems, and in many instances, *with* the Serbs.[14] Much as we might find this sort of behaviour both extraordinary and deplorable, we must remember that the Allies did exactly the same sort of thing in WWII.

* * * * * * * *

With ghastly scenes of violence coming out of Vukovar and elsewhere, the EU rushed to intervene, the Germans (and the Vatican) rushed to support Croatia,[15] and a deal was rushed through in January 1992. In so doing, we no longer recognised the borders of Yugoslavia as inviolable. We had changed our minds. Such are the ways of international diplomacy. Instead, we did three different things: we recognised Croatia as independent because of that referendum;[16] we refused to recognise Bosnia without a referendum; and we decided Kosovo would not be recognised, even though they *had* held a referendum.

---

12   See Glenny, 1992, p 148; Silber and Little, pp 143-4; Thompson , p 322; and Woodward, p 216. The last named suggests such talks took place between Karadžić and Boban as well.

13   See Malcolm, 1996, p 248.

14   Silber and Little, p 205.

15   For the role of the Germans, see in particular Carrington's warning, where he pleaded with Germany not to do anything prematurely; *"I said... that if they recognised Croatia... this would mean a civil war [in Bosnia]."* His pleas were in vain. (Silber and Little, p 220.)
       For the role of the Vatican, see Woodward, p 149. Altogether, all would have been wiser to have adopted the Belfast peace process slogan and to insist that for Yugoslavia too, *"nothing would be agreed until everything was agreed".*

16   In so doing, we recognised the 'right' of a people to determine itself on the basis of a religious, not an ethnic difference, for as noted on p 6, the Croats are Catholic Slavs, the Serbs are Orthodox Slavs. In similar fashion, the world now recognises the right of the East (or Catholic) Timorese to be independent of their ethnic cousins, the West (or Moslem) Timorese.

The first consequence was war in Bosnia. And we just watched it happen. The UN, which was based in Sarajevo for its operations in Croatia, was initially in the embarrassing position of being in a conflict with no mandate at all! So they ran away. Then they returned for humanitarian purposes only, while various diplomats came up with all sorts of proposals and peace-plans, all based on division and majoritarianism.

None of these suggestions worked. Each of the three sides acted as if they had the right of veto, and there was always at least one who exercised that power. As often as not, it was Karadžić, for at that time he was winning the war, and the West was losing the peace-keeping. From a sense of utter frustration, those involved on the ground - primarily the British and the French - started to say they would pull out. And those not so involved - the Americans - said OK you guys, if you do need to get out, we'll help.

* * * * * * * *

Then came that which, in 1945, we had said would never happen again: genocide, Srebrenica. It caused everyone to change their minds, if only for pragmatic reasons. Something had to be done.

It happened again at Žepa. Next would be Goražde. Well, if you were a refugee in Goražde, if you knew you were surrounded by the rebel Bosnian Serbs, and if you knew what had just happened in Srebrenica and Žepa, you would not let the UN go. You would lie down in front of their vehicles, which is what happened. Or you would shoot.

America thus realised that any policy to evacuate UNPROFOR would be very costly, both to themselves and to Bosnia, for there would be many casualties during the evacuation, and then even more casualties in more and more Srebrenicas, in Bihać, Tuzla, Sarajevo, until the entire Moslem population had been wiped out. In the proposed division of Bosnia discussed between Milošević and Tudjman, the former was meant to get 65%, the latter 35%; in effect, one must suppose, the Moslems were due to be 'exiled, killed, or converted'.[17]

Therefore, the Americans *had* to go in. Accordingly, they ditched the UN and called in NATO, for they don't like this democracy stuff - they only ever fight when they are in charge. The effect, on the ground, was simple: lots of UNPROFOR chaps took off their blue berets and put on their khaki ones, and they re-painted all their vehicles from white to camouflage. But, with the notable addition of US forces, it was the same people who were there. To say that the UN was no good and that only NATO could do the necessary was pure propaganda and absolute nonsense. Only at this stage, however, did Karadžić come under any effective pressure; it proved to be crucial.

---

17 A phrase taken from WWII, when Pavelić tried to eliminate all Serbs, a third by each method. Hence the concentration camp at Jasenovac, where Moslems and Roma also died. (See Maclean, p 45 and Glenny, 1999, p 498.)

The Americans have only one peace-keeping military strategy: bombs from the air.[18] Military doctrine, however, says nothing can be achieved by air-power alone, that you also need troops on the ground. Never mind, there was that nice fascist, Tudjman.[19] He would do the dirty work, literally. In August 1995, he ethnically cleansed the Knin *krajina* and then entered Bosnia to do the same, just after NATO bombs had destroyed the ammo dumps and other military facilities of the rebel Bosnian Serbs. Karadžić had now lost; therefore, he gave up his power of veto, and Milošević, who was now the peace-maker, signed a peace agreement. That was Dayton.

* * * * * * * *

We may note that no such pressures were ever applied in Northern Ireland. Karadžić acquired his power by force of arms. The unionists did the same in the 1920s, and while we cannot foist the sins of their fathers onto the present generation of unionist leaders, it is still fair to say that their influence is greater than it should be, and maybe some sort of pressure was required, if ever their position of advantage was to be reduced.

In fact, of course, any pressures for change have been minuscule. This is because, initially, Britain had a strategic, an economic and a political reason for keeping the unionists on board; and while Gorbachev removed the first and the role of multi-nationals has reduced the second, the political advantage inherent in a small clique of unionist politicians remaining at Westminster has remained, or did so until Tony Blair gained such a huge majority of the seats, in 1997.[20] The danger is that it might yet return.

* * * * * * * *

The second consequence of the referendum failures of the EU was Kosova. The province had been unsettled for years, of course, but as usual, international diplomacy had left it until it came to a crisis. As we will see in the next chapter, it came to a head in 1998/9. Rambouillet, however, did not work; maybe, like earlier efforts, it was not meant to work.[21] So NATO came in with the bombs; the KLA were the 'troops on the ground' (even if they had been a bunch of 'terrorists' just months earlier); and 'might was again right'.

---

18 *"Give us bombs for peace,"* said Holbrooke on one famous occasion. Holbrooke, p 132. From a moral point of view, the strategy was exactly the same as that used by the rebel Bosnian Serbs who attacked Sarajevo from the near perfect safety of the surrounding hills.

19 *Ibid*, p 160. Holbrooke's particular advice to Tudjman was as follows: *"Mr. President, I urge you to go as far as you can, but not to take Banja Luka."*

20 The British parliament is one of the few in which certain members have little or no interest in its everyday proceedings - the unionist MPs. As noted on p 10, the latter could easily be 'bought' by either Labour (Callaghan, in 1978) or Conservative (Major on Maastricht in 1996), whenever the government of the day began to lose its majority. In this way, yet again, both the bigger parties managed to bypass the "others", those damned Liberals, who *were* interested in matters British.

21 In October 1998, the international community agreed to send 2,400 unarmed observers to Kosova. It only managed to muster 1,300. Unarmed persons, it seems, are in short supply. There are now some 40,000 armed personnel deployed in that province.

If might had been more right, however, if diplomacy had been rather more prescient... in Northern Ireland, as well as in both Bosnia and Kosova, the large numbers of troops and enormous costs of these deployments could have been much lower. As so often happens, however, international diplomacy is governed by a few individual nations and their own economic considerations. For years, Britain just turned a blind eye to what was going on in Belfast. And for a long time, the West did the same in the Balkans. Furthermore, even when they did act, they were forever trying to do things in the cheapest way possible. It was often a false economy and, as a result, we will be stuck in the Balkans for a long time to come, just as the British have been and still are in Northern Ireland.

At last, however, the international community has agreed to give a commitment to the Balkans, through the July 1999 Stability Pact. Yet still the lessons have not been properly learnt. The main movers in the international community - Britain, France, Germany, Russia and the USA (with the UN by-passed, as usual) - the so-called Contact Group, are pretty well exactly the same players who were involved in that Congress of Berlin, in 1878. We just delete Austria-Hungary, and insert USA. It might be the dawn of a new era, to quote the rhetoric, or it may just be history, repeating itself, yet again.

* * * * * * * *

What a pity we did not have such a concentration of purpose in 1990. At that stage, though, the West was part of the problem. First of all, we were enjoying a standard of living to which many eastern Europeans aspired, and maybe the main reason why the individual republics of Yugoslavia wanted to break away was so that they would be richer.[22] Secondly, with the collapse of communism, the West decided Yugoslavia was no longer important,[23] and flows of western aid dried up while the tide of foreign debt remained. Thirdly, by allowing the international community to be Washington's play-thing, and by not allowing the UN to be a real force of international law, independent of any super-power vetoes and so on, all peace-keeping (in both conflicts) has been subject to petty national interests.

Fourthly, (and here we return to the main subject matter of this book), in the wave of democratisation which swept across eastern Europe after the collapse of the Berlin Wall, we gave to, or imposed upon, the Balkans, a democratic system which was intrinsically divisive and adversarial, and which had already shown itself to be, not part of the solution, but part of the problem in NI. Fifthly, in such statements as the Helsinki Final Act and so forth, we turned international law into an ass. And sixthly, by not defining the so-called right of self-determination - by not specifying more precisely what is a

---

22 Similarly, in NI, the initial arguments related to the UK or rather the British Empire and its relatively strong economy, especially when compared to the old concept of a poverty-ridden Ireland. With to-day's Celtic Tiger, of course, those days are gone.

23 Just as Britain had decided NI was no longer important, strategically, that is, (see p 21).

people, and by allowing a group to determine itself on the basis of only a majority of itself - we exacerbated tensions in these and other divided communities.

When Clauswitz described war as politics by other means, he had in mind an international political system which was based on a rivalry of nations. Exactly the same sort of logic, however, applies to civil war and a democratic system based on the rivalry of political parties.[24] In both Belfast and Yugoslavia, most political parties regard themselves as representing their 'nation', or at least, that part of 'their' nation which is in the present state. Their allegiance is to that nation and not to that state, unless of course the two coincide. As implied on p 16, therefore, their allegiance to any peace process has to be questioned.

For the politicians in Dublin and London, or those in Berlin, London Moscow, Paris and Washington, to think that the traditional, western, adversarial democratic system could be anything but provocative in either conflict was, at best, naïve. If they really wanted peace in Northern Ireland and the Balkans, they would first seek to reform their own democratic structures, so that they too could practice a form of power-sharing, and only then seek to impose. Firstly, therefore, they should read the next two chapters.

---

24 One could say that the political parties themselves - along with the very party political system, its democratic (sic) leaders and party whips and so forth - are actually part of the problem. A possible part of the solution, therefore, is a tripartite reform:

a) a stipulation that all candidates should be independent, i.e., responsible to their constituents only, as is now the case in Uganda;

b) an electoral system designed to ensure that the success of any one candidate depends on the opinions (or votes) of the entire electorate, and not just on those of a quota; and

c) a decision-making process based, not on the first demands of only a majority, but on everybody's best possible compromise.

Alas, what happens in practice is the very opposite. International organisations, governments and such like tend to support, and thereby perpetuate, the existing political parties, and thus the party political system itself. The OSCE, for example, actually gave Arkan, the indicted war criminal Željko Raznatović, £150,000 towards his 1996 election expenses, because he was contesting that election as the leader of a political party. Guardian, 17.1.00.

CHAPTER 4

'DEMOCRACY' - A CAUSE OF WAR

"Would that I did not live in exciting times."

Chinese proverb.

The democratic process consists of two actions: we first elect our chosen representatives, and then either they in parliament or we in national referenda take decisions. In this chapter, we will discuss elections, and we'll leave decision-making until Chapter 5. But before we look at the specific details of the electoral systems which are or could be used in Northern Ireland and the Balkans, let us first examine the effects of our democratic structures, as they exist at the moment.

To any who follow the 'democratic' path to power, there is an easy road to success: you first find and antagonise a minority, for thus you can increase your majority support. Milošević did exactly that in his infamous speech in Kosovo, (p 25). Tudjman did it in Croatia by sacking many Orthodox/Serb civil servants, purely because of their religion/nationality. Hitler did the same, by focusing on the Jews. And Stalin did it by sending a 'minority' of five million *kulaks* to Siberia.[1] It is sobering to reflect that the first three dictators either gained or consolidated their power through the democratic process, and even Joe himself advanced his career by use of the majority vote.

In a word, in most electoral systems, majoritarian or proportional, candidates can increase their own level of support by antagonising those who favour their opponents.

Secondly, it is easier for the unionist or nationalist candidate to canvass in only his/her own areas, whereas those who stand on a non-sectarian ticket are obliged to work throughout the constituency. In similar fashion, the SDP in Bosnia have a much harder task than many another party, for they have to maintain a profile in both entities.

Thirdly, given both the adversarial nature of our politics and the way the media seems to prefer such controversy, parties often tend to concentrate on the negative aspects of their opponents, so people vote, not so much *for* a particular policy or philosophy, but rather *against* that which they don't like. If you, the candidate, suggest dog-licences should be set at £5, you might

---

1   The *kulaks* were the supposedly rich peasants who, it was said, were the 'enemy of the people'. The bolsheviks also believed in majority voting, by the way, but only if and when it suited them. The word 'bolshevik', after all, means majoritarian, from the Russian *'bolshinstvo'* meaning 'majority'.

gain some support; at the same time, however, you might lose the support of all those who would prefer £4, £6, zero, or whatever. It is therefore much easier to criticise the other candidate who says they should be £x, regardless of the value of x, (as long as it's not your own £5). A simple example of this sort of behaviour was evident a few years ago, when pretty well every party in Northern Ireland was standing on a negative ticket: no to SF, said the milder unionists; smash them yelled the DUP; Brits out! rejoined SF; remove the unionist veto, was the SDLP's double negative; and just like the rest of them, the moderate Alliance said no to UDI.

A fourth and final factor relates to the near universal belief in majoritarianism, which is so much a part of Chapter 5's decision-making. But because the politicians tend to boil down every complex question to only two supposed opposites, often evaporating in the process many a sophisticated compromise, the political activists certainly, and sometimes too the people themselves, think in terms of only two alternatives. When things are not Catholic or Protestant, Serb or Croat etc., they become republican or democrat, left or right, or whatever. Societies everywhere, it seems, tend to divide into two. And societies that are already divided into two by religion and/or ethnicity, often find the divided communities themselves are also divided into two.

In Northern Ireland, for example, there are the two main unionist parties, the UUP and the DUP, not to mention all the little dogs like the UKUP, PUP, UDP, and some little dead dogs like the UPNI. The nationalists too have split into two: the SDLP and SF are the main contestants sniffing for political power, with the IRSP and others yapping at their tails. Similarly, in Bosnia, on the Orthodox side, there are the SDS and the SRS, with a plethora of smaller Serb hounds barking in the wings. The Catholics had their splits in the HDZ, but now have the two parties, HDZ and NHI. The Bosnians have their SDA and MBO, amongst others small and not so small. And the Albanians in Kosova have the pacifist Ibrahim Rugova and the militant KLA.

* * * * * * * *

Party politics, then, is a system which is inherently divisive. It is better than war-war, of course, but the jaw-jaw of institutionalised confrontation may not be the only, let alone the best way to resolve differences. At the moment, however, because politicians have their power-base in a system which means their electoral success depends upon the opinions of only *some* voters - as expressed by either the x's of the largest minority or the preferences of a quota - they actually have a vested interest in confrontation.

Furthermore, they will invariably do, first and foremost, that which is necessary to perpetuate their own power base. For example, one of the first measures of the new unionist government in the 1920s was to scrap the proportional representation (PR-STV) electoral system and replace it with the old 'first-past-the-post', for thus they would be able to increase their electoral success. Fianna Fáil tried to do the same down South, but because of the written constitution, they first had to hold a referendum;

the government lost; silly people, they said; so they had another referendum, which again the 'silly people' rejected, this time by an even greater majority.[2] Meanwhile, across the water where there is no written constitution, the English government introduced the 'first-past-the-post' system over a hundred years ago, and in so doing threw out a more sophisticated system.

The above makes it sound as if PR is a good thing. Well, when compared to first-past-the-post, it most certainly is. It does at least ensure that those whom we call our elected representatives include not only the nationalists and unionists, but also some "others". Nevertheless, PR is still adversarial,[3] and a more inclusive system would suggest the success of any candidate should depend on the opinions (i.e., preferences) of every voter in the constituency, and not just on those of a fraction. More of all that at the end of the chapter.

* * * * * * * *

First, however, we return to the Balkans which, as a result of the collapse of communism in 1989, came under the tide of multi-party elections which swept across eastern Europe, from East Germany and even into Albania. They were indeed exciting times.[4]

Now in 1974, we remember, Tito wrote a new constitution[5] for the FRY, and tried thereby to consolidate a form of power-sharing which would survive his death. In retrospect, we can say it was a fair effort. There were, however, a number of mistakes, which had enormous repercussions.

Firstly, the joint presidency was meant to work by consensus, a phrase taken to mean unanimity. The system therefore gave each republic the power of veto. When such a power exists, sooner or later, I'm afraid, one or other participant will use it... and then there will be an *impasse*. For a 'multi-multi' society like that of Northern Ireland or Yugoslavia, such a consociational system is far superior to any simple majoritarianism. Better an *impasse,* and further discussion, than a majoritarian tyranny.

Secondly, there was the question of whether or not elections should be held at the Federal level or in each separate Republic, and which were to be superior. By 1991, when the question was raised, it was too late, for Slovenia vetoed, and the moment was lost.

---

2   The government lost the first referendum by 51.8%; that was in 1959. Their second attempt came nine years later, when they lost by 61%! Not to be outdone, Fianna Fáil is now considering another change.

3   This is especially true when the threshold is quite high. Under PR-STV in a 3-seater constituency, the threshold is 25%; in a 4-seater, it's 20%. With some forms of PR-List, it may be as little as 0.7%, as in the Netherlands, and therefore far less adversarial.

4   Slovenia and Croatia held their first multi-party elections in April, Macedonia and Bosnia in November, Montenegro and Serbia in Dec, 1990.

5   *"The longest such document in the world,"* Glenny, 1999, p 593.

THE DE BORDA INSTITUTE

Thirdly, Tito gave recognition to the Bosnian Moslems. That, in itself, was not a mistake of course. As we noted earlier, Yugoslavia had started as The Kingdom of Serbs, Croats and Slovenes, and no recognition at all had been given to any of the other groupings. But by now allowing some of those others to call themselves Moslems (and not Bosniaks), he had fallen prey to that Serb/Croat propaganda we mentioned, for it inferred that Bosnia was not on an equal par with Croatia or Serbia.[6]

One can only compare like with like. Either you describe people by their religious affiliation or by their Republic of residence... or by age, size or whatever. You cannot, however, describe one phenomenon by two different criteria, without getting into a lot of trouble. Some consequences are obvious: the Albanian Moslem had a choice of identities, as opposed to the Albanian Catholic; as noted in the glossary (p vii), many residents of the Sandžak are both Serb and Moslem, yet many residents regard the two labels as either/or; and numerous Bosnians were unable to identify themselves properly with Bosnia, because both those words 'Croat' and 'Serb', like those two other adjectives 'British' and 'Irish', relate to external centres of power.

Finally, given these three factors, the introduction of any western form of democracy was bound to make it easier for the separatist. Just as the sectarian candidate need canvass in only one part of the constituency, (p 31), so too it was much easier for the Slovenian politician to advocate independence rather than work for the continuation of the FRY. A charismatic Tito could lead an entire Yugoslavia; anyone of a lesser stature, as needless to say all subsequent members of the presidency were almost bound to be, might not be able to. There was one who could have managed, if but other factors both internal and international had been more favourable, and that was Ante Marković, affectionately known as the last Yugoslav. Alas, as we shall see, his efforts were in vain.

THE ELECTIONS

If you change the electoral system, different persons may get elected. This was demonstrated very clearly in Northern Ireland in 1996, when the British government concocted a most unusual two-part system, because they wanted not only the usual 'old faces' to be elected, but also those politicians who represented the Protestant paramilitaries. They therefore chose a d'Hondt[7] PR-List system in which voters could choose only a party, and then

---

6   The change was gradual. In 1942, the communists recognised five nationalities: Serbs, Croats, Slovenes, Macedonians and Montenegrins. In the 1948 census, folks were able to express their religion (Orthodox, Catholic or Moslem) and nationality (Moslem, undetermined). In 1953, the question of religion was no longer present, and Bosnians could now opt for one of three nationalities: Serb, Croat, Yugoslav or undetermined.

7   d'Hondt is a divisor system which works fairly well, as long as it is held in large, multi-member constituencies. In this instance, they were held in tiny 5-seater constituencies - the smallest size for a d'Hondt election held anywhere since 1945, (see Lijphart, 1994, p 22). Needless to say,

34

added not a 'top-up' but a 'top-down' part, in which the top ten parties would gain an extra two seats each, regardless of how many seats they had already won in the first part. Sure enough, both the PUP and the UDP got their two seats. But given that the chosen form of PR was this d'Hondt count in those tiny 5-seater constituencies, the system favoured the four or five biggest parties. Then came the second part, which favoured the ten biggest parties. That electoral system might have been free;[8] it certainly was not fair.

Since then, the local politicians have gone back to PR-STV, the chosen form of PR which as we said had been part of the 1920 Act of Settlement and which was re-introduced into Northern Ireland in 1972 under direct rule. The fact that is extraordinary in all this, however, is two-fold: firstly, most of those who believe in the principle of proportionality in elections nevertheless believe in majoritarianism in decision-making; people can have preferences when electing representatives, apparently, but those same people and/or their representatives in parliament cannot have preferences on matters of policy and, equally apparently, they must all return to the primitive 'for-or-against' of majority rule. There is no logic whatsoever to that position.

Secondly, PR is still adversarial. As we said on p 16, a candidate needs only a quota. PR-STV is a good system, for it allows the voter who so wishes to exercise his/her preferences across the sectarian divide. Unfortunately, however, such an act of *rapprochement* is not fully recognised in the counting procedure, for either that vote helps to get a candidate elected, or, as we noted in fn5 on p 3, it is *transferred,* literally, to another candidate; this is definitely the case when the voter's first preference candidate is eliminated, and is partially true when a first preference candidate is elected with a surplus. Unfortunately, however, the Belfast peace process failed to even consider any more inclusive systems, and those who had so often been elected under PR-STV knew well enough that if they kept to this system, they would probably be re-elected.

PR-STV has some other disadvantages as well. Briefly, it is designed to benefit the bigger parties and, in a four-seater constituency for example, where the quota is 20% of the valid vote, any party with less than that may well be unsuccessful. More importantly, however, is the fact that the hypothetical candidate who is the second preference of everybody but the first preference of none - i.e., the perfect compromise - will get a first round score of zero! PR-STV, therefore, might have been of no use at all to Ante Marković.

---

therefore, such an extraordinary system produced some extraordinary results: SF, for example, got twice as many votes as the SDLP in West Belfast - 22,355 votes to 11,087 - but four times as many seats!

8   It was 'free' in so far as the average punter was able to exercise a secret vote; it was not 'free' if, by that term, we refer to the ability of a voter to choose whomsoever he/she wishes, for each was only able to vote only for a party, not for a candidate; furthermore, each was allowed only one preference.

It must be emphasised that the vote is indeed transferable: so, as I say, those who vote for both Protestant *and* Catholic may well find their vote is transferred from one to the other, and thus it helps to elect *either* one *or* the other! In a Quota Borda System, on the other hand, the voter can be truly pluralist, and help both.[9]

* * * * * * * *

Yugoslavia's first post-communist multi-party elections took place in 1990. As we said a moment ago, Slovenia vetoed any idea of an all-Yugoslav election because Ljubljana was already hell-bent on independence, regardless of the consequences for anyone else in the Federation.

In theory, elections should represent the popular will. This might be the case if the electoral system is fair, but it also depends on the occasion. In this particular instance, however, *"The demand for elections did not originate from popular pressure, but with politicians seeking more political power over their territories..."*[10]

Furthermore, it was these same politicians who selected the electoral system. Unlike Slovenia which had a form of PR, Croatia chose a two-round majority vote system, similar in many ways to the French and British majoritarian systems. The consequences were just what Tudjman wanted. *"The HDZ got 1.2 million votes to 1.0 million for the reformed communists. But Croatia's British style first-past-the-post, single member constituency electoral system gave Tudjman's party an absolute majority of the seats in the new [parliament], even though it had won fewer than half the votes cast in the country. Small parties were weeded out."*[11] The mathematics are pretty horrible: he got 42% of the vote, 68% of the seats, and 100% of the power. Ah well, Thatcher did the same with only 44% of the vote; who are we (democrats) to complain?

In Serbia, the story is much the same. *"Less than half the electorate voted"* - Kosovo, for instance, boycotted anything which enhanced the Belgrade administration - yet Milošević *"garnered 52% of the votes,"* 78% of the seats in parliament, and again, 100% of the power.[12] This election was actually witnessed by the late James Kilfedder MP, the member for North Down, who went out to Serbia along with lots of other international observers, to see if the elections were fair. And yes they were, he said. What else could a majoritarian say?[13]

---

9 For a full critique of PR-STV, see Emerson, 1998.

10 Woodward, p 117.

11 Silber and Little, p 96. Yet at no stage do these authors suggest a better system.

12 Thompson, p 212. He, too, offers no better alternative. The Kosovo boycott, needless to say, was adhered to by the Albanians but not by the Serbs. In 1991, this led to what must surely be an undemocratic world record: the election of Serjdo Bajramović on only 0.03% of the votes! (See Malcolm, 1996, p 224.)

13 In 1979, Thatcher got 44% of the vote, 53% of the seats, and 100% of the power. In 1983, she got

Bosnia, of course, is different. Slovenia was most definitely a state in which there were no major internal ethnic differences. Croatia consisted mainly, but only mainly, of Croats; there were some Italians in Istra and some Serbs in the *krajina* (with even more Serbs in Zagreb, but unlike their *krajina* cousins, the city Serbs did not form a local majority).[14] And Serbia consisted of many Serbs but also of many other peoples, not just the Albanians in Kosova, but also the Moslems in Sandžak, and the Croats, Hungarians, Czechs, Slovaks, etc., in Vojvodina.

Bosnia, however, was a multi-multi society. There was no one group which could claim to have a majority. The people were, roughly and nominally, 40% Moslem, 30% Orthodox, and 20% Catholic, to use the same hopelessly inaccurate criteria which everyone else uses. Before those first elections in 1990, Bosnia was at peace with itself, more or less. The introduction of a divisive, western-style election ruined whatever internal harmony they had, for it allowed those parties with a nationalist agenda to then dominate the political landscape; indeed, it paved the way for division and war.

"*Driving across Bosnia in 1990 just prior to the elections afforded me a brief glimpse into the republic's miserable future. One village drowning in a sea of green crescents, (Moslem)... would give way to another where... the HDZ was sovereign, or where every wall was covered with the acronym SDS. In some villages, the western half was green while the eastern half was red, white and blue (Serbian)... Many doomed settlements were a jumble of all three. This deeply entangled demography would ensure that if terror and war were to break out in any region of Yugoslavia, the pressure on the three communities in Bosnia-Herzegovina to fight would be overwhelming.*"[15]

Before those elections, as I say, people were living fairly well together... and I quote just one story. On the eve of the elections, a family sat down to dinner and discussed what they would do. Like so many other families in Bosnia, it was a mixed marriage, and the three adults considered not only those politicians who stood for sectional interests, but also those who stood on a cross-community platform. One such was Ante Marković.

He "*was the most popular politician in all of Yugoslavia during the spring of 1990, above Kučan, Tudjman and Milošević... [and many] looked increasingly to Marković as their only hope against the republican leaders and parliaments and the consequences of social disintegration.*"[16] This

---

only 42% of the vote, but 62% of the seats! And in 1997, New Labour and all that, Blair got 44% of the vote and 64% of the seats! Meanwhile, in 1979, the Liberals got 14% of the vote for 1.7% of the seats; in 1983, 25% of the vote gave them 3.5% of the seats; and in 1997, 17% of the vote produced 7% of the seats! Doubtless again, both Milošević and Tudjman would say, oh yes, that's all very fair.

14   Thompson, p 283.

15   Glenny, 1992, pp 146-7.

16   Woodward, p 128.

family was amongst that number, and they all decided to give their vote to Markovic's Reform League. Such a decision was typical, and *"trends identified by many observers and public opinion polls... indicated that voters would support parties espousing non-ethnic or cross-ethnic programmes"*.[17]

One day later, they sat down together again. Well dear, pass the butter would you, which way did you vote? And of the three, only one voted for Markovic. The other two both said they felt they had to vote first (?) for 'one of their own'.

If the system had been different, if the voters had been allowed to use preferences, and If then all of those preferences had all been taken into account, maybe the result would have been different. Maybe, too, the consequences of that election would have been different. Maybe, different people would have been elected, and maybe the war could have been avoided. Why is it, then, that people give such little thought to the choice of electoral system? And why do we leave it to the politicians themselves to decide what system the voters will have, whether the latter like it or not?

In Bosnia's two-round electoral system, Markovic won only 13 of the 240 parliamentary seats, while the reformed communists gained just 18. In contrast, among the three nationalist parties, the SDA won 87, the SDS 71 and HDZ 44. As if those results were not bad enough in themselves, the even more disheartening fact is that these three *"had secretly agreed before the elections to form a coalition government"*.[18]

This they now did, establishing a joint presidency and a consociational form of government in which, in effect, each of the three 'nations' - Moslem, Orthodox and Catholic - had the power of veto. *"In its eighteen-month-long existence, the Bosnia parliament failed to pass a single law"*.[19] As happens so often in history, the gang of thieves argued amongst themselves; shortly afterwards, they plunged the country into war.

The point, however, is this: a bad electoral system can cause the wrong people to be elected. Therefore, the choice of electoral system should not be left to the politicians alone. Instead, the people themselves should decide, based on certain guidelines in such as the United Nations Charter on Human Rights, which should state which systems are acceptable, and which are not. Alas, of course - and here we are back to the three old men, Churchill, Roosevelt and Stalin - it does nothing of the kind.

* * * * * * * *

Both Croatia and Bosnia have since changed their electoral systems. Croatia has adopted what might sound rather nice: a part majoritarian

---

17 Cohen, p 146.

18 Silber and Little, p 232. Yet again, antagonists do not like any "others".

19 Glenny, 1992, p 148.

and part PR system. Unlike the German MMP system, however, in which the PR part counters any disproportionate results obtained in the first part, Croatia's two parts are totally separate, and therefore the overall result will probably not be proportional. Furthermore, as another measure of their democratic credibility, 6% of the seats are reserved for eight different minority groups: Hungarians, Italians, Czechs, Slovaks, Ruthenians, Ukrainians, Germans and Austrians - which does not help the Serbs very much![20]

Bosnia, meanwhile, is the subject of Dayton, an agreement which did not specify the electoral system to be used. Any elections, it insisted, had to be *"free and fair"*, but that stipulation applied not so much to the choice of system, rather to the conditions in which the elections were to take place. The punter, in other words, had to be able to go to the polling station and vote, without any harassment; in a land of over two million displaced persons, that was quite a tall order.

The actual specifics of the electoral system, however, were not resolved until later. Sadly, to put it mildly, the methodologies chosen by the OSCE were very unfair. In the presidential elections, for example, a Bosnian refugee from Srebrenica, now living in Tuzla but wishing (at some stage) to return there, was entitled to vote as a citizen of that town. His choice in the presidential election, however, was limited, and he/she was able to vote for either a bad or a worse Serb member of the presidency, and not at all for whatever sort of Croat or Bosniak candidate. In effect, therefore, the electoral system was a form of 'democratic ethnic cleansing'.

Meanwhile, in the *RS* presidential elections (as opposed to the B-H presidentials), a non-Serb *could* stand. In 1998, there was one such candidate, so while the voters of *RS* elected an SDS candidate for the B-H presidency, exactly the same people voting in exactly the same way elected an SRS person, Poplašen, to the *RS* presidency, because by then, the vote was split. The count was majoritarian, and he 'won', with only 44% of the vote. Nothing wrong with that, of course, Thatcher might again say.

A further change to the electoral system has now been recommended by the National Working Group (NWG), under Prof. Nadžer Milićević. This was set up in December 1998 by the Madrid meeting of the Peace Implementation Council to review the PR-List system initiated after Dayton. The draft electoral law suggests presidential elections will be under AV, while parliamentary assemblies will be elected via a two-tier PR-List system.[21]

---

20   IDEA, 1997, p 98.

21   The author met Prof. Milićević twice in Jan 1999 and, in a formal presentation to a full meeting of the NWG, argued for QBS. According to the professor whom he met again in July, it *might* have been adopted if Bosnia had already been equipped with electronic counting. Given, however, that the NWG consisted of persons representing their own 'ethnic' groups, it is sad but hardly surprising that the draft electoral law advocates an electoral system which, though better than its predecessor, still perpetuates the party system.

Despite repeated submissions, QBS was not considered at all during the Belfast Talks.

QUOTA BORDA SYSTEM (QBS)

Proportionality is very important, not only in divided societies, and one advantage of a truly proportional system is that it allows the voters themselves to decide what are the important issues. If a quota decides that somebody should be elected because he/she is a Catholic, Protestant, Bosniac, Croat or Serb, they should indeed be able to choose such a candidate. If another quota wants a female representative, they should have one. Or if a quota wants to raise a particular issue which the parties have not covered, be it on nuclear power or whatever, again, they should be able to do so. Such are the advantages of both PR-STV and QBS, but not of other forms of PR like some PR-List systems.

QBS has a number of other advantages. Firstly, it means the voter can effect a measure of reconciliation by giving some points to a Protestant *and* some to a Catholic, some to a Bosniac *and* some to a Serb *and* again some too to a Croat, if such is their wish, for the count will ensure *both* or *all* candidates benefit from such a vote.[22] Secondly, it means the success of a candidate may indeed depend upon the wishes of every voter in that constituency. This is the inclusive principle, from which so much else flows.[23]

When societies elect politicians who have an obligation to all their constituents and not just some of them, when the elected representatives involved in peace talks have the wishes of society as a whole as their primary objective, and when the chosen methodology of decision-making is no longer a win-or-lose battle, then might the situation in both Belfast and Bosnia be more conducive to co-operation and compromise.

It might be even better when those elected have only one obligation as a result of their election, namely, to their constituents. This could happen if and when, as in Uganda (see p 30, fn) and Nunavut,[24] political parties as such are not allowed to participate in elections; instead, every candidate has to be independent, with no-one exercising any whips upon them.

Such a system is quite feasible, however, even without a ban on political parties, but to make it work, decision-making in parliaments would have to be based on a free, multi-option voting procedure. It's time for the next page.

---

22 In this respect, QBS is so very different from PR-STV; see p 35.

23 *"Proportionality [was] achieved in Lebanon by forcing each voter to cast his votes for candidates belonging to different sects in proportion to the sectarian composition of each electoral district."* Lijphart in *Consociation: The Model and its Applications in Divided Societies,* (see p 55 fn), p 177. As far as I know, this is the only occasion when voters in a divided society have been *"forced"* to vote for others apart from 'their own'. PR-STV in Northern Ireland *allows* those who so wish to vote across the divide. QBS, on the other hand, actually *encourages* the voter to do so.

24 The newly autonomous territory in Canada.

CHAPTER 5

A DECISION ON DECISION-MAKING

"I never knew that there were a million Germans in Bohemia."

President Woodrow Wilson,
the architect of the so-called *"right of self-determination"*
in later, reflective mood.[1]

We come to the climax of this booklet. There are some fairly good electoral systems in this world, some pretty bad ones, and occasionally a bit of a debate about it all. On decision-making, however, almost every political institution uses the worst decision-making process ever invented - apart, that is, from the duel - the straight, two-option, majority vote.

When it was invented, I know not. Maybe it was devised by the ancient Greeks; perhaps it originated earlier. What we do know is this: it is primitive, divisive, and hopelessly inaccurate. Secondly, as we said earlier, it forces people to take sides, and thus it can be a cause of war. Thirdly, just as peace talks sometimes exclude the right people, so too the majority vote, in effect, often disenfranchises the most peaceful people, those who would otherwise want to vote for compromise, the moderate, the children of a mixed marriage, the "others", the progressive, and the *"ethnically unclean"*.

Why, then, do people continue to use this lousy system, especially in contentious national plebiscites? The answer, I'm afraid, is horribly simple: because politicians the world over, though they say they want democracy, want first of all to control the agenda; (see p 10). Some of them, admittedly, have actually been brought up to think that majoritarianism is OK. Some are blissfully unaware of even the existence of other voting methodologies. And all are joined by a chorus of intellectuals, from historians to political scientists and journalists, who also say they believe in this shibboleth.

* * * * * * * *

Just as a bad electoral system has certain advantages for those politicians who thereby get elected (and who would not be so successful if the system was fairer), so too a bad decision-making process, the majority vote, has one huge advantage for those who practice it. It enables them, as I say, to control the agenda. Brilliant; that's just what they want. And the thing that is most brilliant of all, from their point of view, is that people not only *think*, but actually *believe* it is democratic.

---

1   Quoted in *Diplomacy for the Next Century* by Abba Eban, Yale University Press, 1998, p 38.

Take, for example, a vote on the electoral system. The Italians had one a few years ago, in the belief that their existing system, a PR-List variant, was a cause of much corruption. They voted 'for-or-against', i.e., *either* for a more majoritarian system *or* for the *status quo*. Therefore, any person who wanted to vote for PR-STV, say, or QBS, or a Swedish-style two-tier system, was at a loss, and the result produced only a certain amount of information: *B* was preferred to *A*. What they thought about *C* or *D*, we still don't know. They nevertheless adopted *B*, the more majoritarian model; they thought they had made a democratic decision; and they finished up with a bunch of neo-fascists![2]

In 1992, New Zealand used a much better methodology: they first held a multi-option vote on five possible electoral systems, i.e., four new PR possibilities and the *status quo*, the old British 'first-past-the-post' system. Collectively, more people wanted change than did not. So they then held a binding vote between what appeared to be the most popular new system and the existing one, and sure enough, it was the more popular. Perfect? Well, that decision-making system was certainly much better; at least the people had a choice![3]

Elsewhere, politicians continue to control the agenda, (and 'independent' commissions like the one chaired by Lord Jenkins also exercise excessive power by extending the agenda to only a minimal degree).[4] What's more, in a two-party democracy or in any other contest, the two big dogs co-operate to keep out the little ones. Like the Croats and Serbs who don't like Moslems, like the Protestant and Catholic churches which don't like integrated education, the two major parties in such a situation will invariably combine to squeeze out any "others".

In England, for example, both Labour and Tory parties co-operated for years in an unholy alliance to exclude the Liberals - much to the delight of the unionists, (see p 28). And Lord Jenkins has now devised a new electoral system which is specifically designed to allow the UK to move from a two-party state to a three-party state but not to a four-party or multi-party state. He is, after all, a liberal. Do as you have been done by, he might say, and he now seeks to squeeze out the Green, and any other sort of "other".

In Northern Ireland terms, such a habit is at least unfortunate, especially when the unionists and nationalists combine to exclude the non-sectarian; and the Alliance party, which claims that label, then tries to

---

2   On 9.6.91, in a 62% turnout, 95% voted in favour of a system in which they had less choice! In the former PR-List system, each could vote for up to four candidates; now they can vote for only one.

3   In the first non-binding vote, in a 55% turnout, only 15% wanted the *status quo*; of those asking for change, 77% opted for a German system, MMP. Come the second binding vote between MMP and the *status quo*, 54% of an 83% turnout chose MMP.

4   Though his report mentioned New Zealand's change of electoral system, it completely ignored both the methodology used, and at least one submission which referred to that mutli-option vote procedure.

squeeze out any others who might aspire to that middle ground: the NILP that was, the Green Party which is, and now the Women's Coalition as well.

Meanwhile, as we already know, Bosnia's three nationalistic parties joined forces to squeeze out any non-sectarian 'other' like Ante Marković.

* * * * * * * *

We are, may I remind the reader, discussing decision-making, which is, of course, quite different from the topic of electoral systems. Admittedly, voting may be used in both. The former, however, leads to only one outcome; the latter may produce a number of winners. The reason why both appear in this chapter is because, unfortunately, the only use of a non-binding multi-option vote on decision-making was the instance we mentioned in New Zealand, where the topic was electoral systems. Multi-option votes have been used in a binding mode, however, on a number of occasions: in Sweden on nuclear power, in Finland on prohibition, and the record stands in Guam, which held a seven-option ballot.[5]

Despite the inherent weaknesses of using two-option majority votes in decision-making, the world still believes in this procedure. In national parliaments and/or international fora, its use is widespread... and hardly ever questioned. But before we discuss those individual referenda which have been a cause of increased tensions if not indeed of war, we must again refer to International Law. For therein lies *"the stark contradiction that quickly emerged between two central articles of the Helsinki Final Act: the commitment to the self-determination of nations; and the principle of the inviolability of borders".*[6]

Given that contradiction, governments find it very easy to vacillate. In 1990, for example, *"Yugoslav territorial integrity and independence [had been] a matter of strategic interest to the West"*. In 1991, as we said in Chapter 4, we began to change our minds, and the European parliament passed a particularly ambiguous resolution to this effect: *"the constituent republics and autonomous provinces of Yugoslavia must have the right freely to determine their own future... on the basis of recognised international and internal borders".*[7] And one year later, we completed the change and recognised Croatia as an independent nation.

But if it involves a choice of only two options, when in fact more than two exist, a straight majority vote cannot be *free*. Politicians and constitutional lawyers argue at length over borders, historical claims,

---

5   This was in 1982, when the Guamese had a choice of six suggested constitutional options, or even a seventh, their own. Now that is what I call pluralism! Some other plurality votes are mentioned in fn4 on p 3.

6   Silber and Little, p 161

7   Woodward, pp 106 and 158.

international treaties and so forth; but they never pause to ask if a choice of only two options is actually *free,* or is it instead restricted.

* * * * * * * *

Let us now look at the specific instances where the referendum has been used, to see how useless it is, and we'll return to that word 'free' in a minute or two. First of all, as usual in these pages, we will look at the simple history in Northern Ireland where, apart from the 1975 vote on joining the Common Market - a vote which was widely interpreted as a vote for peace - there have been just two referenda in the provinoc directly associated with the troubles.

The first was the border poll of 1973. As originally laid down in the legislation, such a ballot was to take place every ten years, until at last peace would reign, for *"it would be appropriate,"* the then Prime Minister stated, *"for the views of the people of NI to be made known on this question from time to time."*[8] The specific question was to ask the voters whether or not they wanted to retain the border. It was a simple, yes-or-no vote. As always, the majority would win; the majority therefore voted. And the minority would lose; therefore they abstained. Indeed, the SDLP called the whole thing *"an exercise in cynicism"* and organised a boycott.[9]

Northern Ireland at the time consisted of about 60% Protestants and 40% Catholics, or so said those intelligent statisticians who regard everyone as either 'this' or 'that', with not even a Chinese carry-out to dilute the dichotomy. The vote took place on 8th March: the turn-out was 59% - i.e., all the Protestants - and the majority in favour was a good, Stalinist 97%. In other words, that vote told us only what we already knew. It achieved nothing, or rather, nothing positive; if anything, it only exacerbated tensions in society, as do so many expressions of the democratic process in this province! At least, the lesson was learnt... or was it? The exercise was not repeated ten years later. Instead, the whole thing was just quietly dropped... until resurrected in the Belfast Agreement.

A second very different referendum was held in 1998. This was not the usual 'black-versus-white' vote of one extreme against its opposite; rather, it was a vote for a compromise, or rather, *the* compromise, with both extremes, the DUP and RSF, 'united' in unholy opposition.

In an unusually high 81% turnout, 71% supported the accord, and 29% opposed.[10] The trouble with an inaccurate measure of opinion, of course,

---

8   Mr. (now Sir) Edward Heath, Hansard 24.3.72, col. 1862. Did he really think the folks would change their minds? Did he actually believe that only two views were possible? And did he and others really think such a procedure would *"take the border out of politics"?*

9   See *The Belfast Telegraph* of 8.3.73, page 4. Even some journalists agreed, the Irish Independent, for example, describing the referendum as *"potentially bitter, divisive and utterly useless..."*

10 Meanwhile, in the Republic on a 56% turnout, 94% voted in favour.

is that such results are open to numerous interpretations. Of the 29%, maybe some of them supported Mr. Paisley; and/or perhaps some supported O'Bradaigh; and maybe a few supported neither. The said Mr. Paisley, however, being like Tudjman, the committed majoritarian (when it suits him), nevertheless tried to claim that he represented a majority of the majority, even though that 29% was such a relatively small minority of society as a whole.

The first figure, 71%, is equally vague. Some of those who voted 'yes' doubtless thought the agreement was very good. Others, myself included, considered that in some aspects, it was appalling, especially in the way it institutionalised and thereby perpetuated sectarian attitudes. We'll take a closer look at this aspect of the agreement in the next chapter. Nevertheless, I voted 'yes', for to do so I surmised was better than voting 'no'. How much nicer it would have been, however, if the people themselves had been given a choice on certain aspects of the agreement, especially those on which the politicians themselves had found it so difficult to agree.

In other words, the final referendum could have offered not just one, but a number of compromise options. A major sticking point in the Talks had been the question of decision-making. Accordingly, the people could have been given a choice of either a consociational method of decision-making, as in the present Belfast Agreement, or, let us say, a less sectarian methodology based on the Borda preferendum. Similarly, on the subject of an electoral system where again there had been some dissent on the detail, the people could have been given a choice: PR-STV in six-seaters; PR-STV in five-seaters; or PR-STV in five-seaters with a province-wide top-up.

Sadly, it seems, the politicians do not wish the people to have such a high level of democratic decision-making.

* * * * * * * *

The Good Friday Agreement lays down the criteria for other referenda. But first, as promised, let me discuss what happened in Quebec, where they had a vote on independence in 1980. It was a contest between some of the French-speaking folk and some of the 'opposition', the English speaking populace. The former lost.

So they waited for a few years, to then have another go. By 1995, Parizeau was the man in charge, and he devised a question to match. Now the opinion pollsters were doing their usual work, and indications were that he was going to lose. He therefore changed the question slightly, to make it sound a little softer, to woo perhaps a few doubters.

He had not changed his mind, however. As mentioned earlier, the majority vote allows he who sets the question almost a total monopoly on the political agenda. And changing the question without changing your intent is blatant manipulation. He lost. It was only by a whisper, but nevertheless, he lost: 50.6% to 49.4%.

We can therefore accuse him of only attempted manipulation. In defeat, Parizeau blamed *"the ethnic vote"* - of which, read on - thereby to confirm that, as suspected, he hadn't changed his mind at all!

He lost, I said. But did he? Or will they wait again for a few more years and then have yet another go? Is the referendum just a *"never-end-'em"*, to quote some wit on BBC Radio 4? After all, that was what the Irish did on the issue of divorce, and so too, the Danish held a second vote on Maastricht.[11]

A further aspect of the Quebec story is also quite interesting from the point of view of the ethnic voters, the Cree Indians. They, of course, had been as it were disenfranchised by such a French-versus-English debate, so they had organised their own referendum just prior to the official one, and sure enough, a majority of them had voted to stay in Canada, 96% no less! Better the devil you know, of course.

* * * * * * * *

We now return to Northern Ireland and the Belfast Agreement, an article of which stipulates that a referendum may be held, every seven years or so, on whether or not Northern Ireland should *either* remain in the United Kingdom *or* become part of a United Ireland. Yet again, it is 'yes-or-no', 'either/or'. Yet again, it is to be repeated every so often. So I'm afraid, the lessons of 1973 have not been learnt at all, and nor have those of Quebec. We too are to have a *"never-end-'em"*.[12]

At the moment, there are about 50% Protestants, 40% Catholics and 10% "other". Not that the last named matter very much, in any majority vote, (but see p 10). The balance between the two denominations may change. In *x* years from now, if present trends continue, an as yet unborn Seamus will have his eighteenth birthday, and the Catholics/nationalists will outnumber the Protestants/unionists by 50% + 1. A referendum, they will demand. Indeed, Bertie Ahern the *Taoiseach* has already asked for one. And yet again, it is 'win-or-lose', no compromise, no *rapprochement*, no nothing, just victory or defeat. 50% + 1 is a majority, of course, and such a total will mean a nationalist victory will be all but guaranteed. Unless Sammy gets his gun and shoots a Taig or two, any Taigs will do, for then it will be 50% - 1, and Northern Ireland will stay in the UK!

It sounds ridiculous, but that is the scenario painted. The peace process has actually laid the seeds of future conflict. Yet the whole world sings its praises.

What is also extraordinary is the use of language. Just as military men use such terms as *"collateral damage"* as a euphemistic cover-up for the murder of maybe countless innocents, so too our politicians change the use of

---

11   The Irish held two votes on divorce, in 1980 and 1995; the Danes held two on the Maastricht Treaty, in 1992 and '93. In both instances, the majority first said 'no', and then a majority said 'yes'; only a few, however, had actually changed their minds!

12   *Op. cit.* Section 1, Annex A, Schedule 1.

certain terms. *'Consent'*, for example, used to mean the agreement of both or all parties, be it to a marriage, a business contract, a political accord or an international treaty. Politically, however, it means the agreement of maybe as few as 50% + 1. This is only because the politicians concerned refuse to consider any other decision-making process.

The two governments have agreed that collectively, we must be *either* British *or* Irish. They too insist we cannot be "other", neither neither nor both. Individually, we can have two passports and so on; that, after all, is easy enough. But collectively, we are not allowed to vote for compromise; we are not allowed to even consider an Anglo-Celtic Federation, or whatever. We may have a British-Irish Council, and one is catered for in the Agreement. But the two national governments, it seems, must remain sovereign, separate, (together in the EU), and superior to any supposedly international body such as that Council. Furthermore, they must continue to rule by majority vote. To change all that, it seems, would be beyond the price of peace.

* * * * * * * *

And so to the Balkans, where the history of the referendum is sadder by far. A full list is in Annex I, but we will consider the detail of only the worst of them, starting with Croatia. There are parallels both with the Irish story, (see p 8), and with what happened in Quebec. For just as the Cree Indians held their separate vote, so too the *krajina* Serbs held theirs, on 12.5.91. Their proposal was to stay in Yugoslavia. The population was overwhelming Serb. The turn-out was 95%. And the result was a majority of 90% in favour.

This *krajina* vote pre-emptied the Croatian poll by just one week. The latter consisted of two questions. The first was this: *"Do you agree that the Republic of Croatia as a sovereign and independent state, which guarantees cultural autonomy and all civil rights to Serbs and members of other nationalities in Croatia, may enter into an alliance with other republics?"* It was, therefore, a bit of a nonsense, for it assumed Croatia was already independent. Tudjman, therefore, was bound to win. Indeed, he had won already! Admittedly, the second question might have clarified matters: *"Are you in favour of the republic of Croatia remaining in Yugoslavia as a federal state?"*

84% voted; 93% (or 92% on the second question) supported whatever they thought they were voting for. And the consequence was also predictable. These two referenda, in *krajina* and Croatia - both equally democratic, in theory, although only one was to be recognised by the international community - were mutually exclusive; by August of that year, the two peoples were at war.

* * * * * * * *

The EC had set up a body called the Badinter Commission, named after the constitutional lawyer who was its head, to resolve any sovereignty disputes in what was still Yugoslavia. It too refused to question the use of the simple majority vote or referendum. Instead, it believed in it to the very letter - with but the one proviso, (see below) - and invited all republics in Yugoslavia to have such a vote, if indeed they wanted to gain independence. Croatia, we know, had already done so, as too had Slovenia.

* * * * * * * *

"Now the EC committed a cardinal error. It recognised Slovenia and Croatia, but not [Bosnia]."[13] Bosnia, which had not yet held a referendum, was told to do so; and this in a land, as we said, of 40%, 30% and 20%, Moslem, Orthodox and Catholic respectively. So no one lot had a majority. As always the very vote forced people to take sides. Given the recent war in Croatia, it was obvious that the Orthodox and Catholic Bosnians would oppose each other; and given the very nature of the problem, the Moslems were not going to side with the Orthodox. Therefore, as was noted on p 26, they joined with the Croats, despite the fact that Tudjman had just organised a coup in Herzegovina, to replace the pro-Bosnian Bosnian Croat leader, Stjepan Kljujić, by the pro-Croat 'Bosnian Croat', Mate Boban.

To be fair to the Badinter Commission, it did lay down that one proviso we mentioned, namely that any outcome would be valid *"only if respectable numbers from all three communities of the republic approved"* that result.[14] And to be fair to the Bosnian government, at least the question was less ambiguous: *"Are you for a sovereign and independent Bosnia and Herzegovina, a state of equal citizens..."* etc..

In the event, as they'd said they would, the rebel Bosnian Serbs boycotted the referendum - the turnout was 63% - just as the SDLP boycotted the 1973 NI border poll, just as the Albanians in Macedonia boycotted that independence referendum as well. In some majority votes, there is absolutely no point in voting if you know you are in the minority. Actually, there is often not much point in voting if you are in the majority either, if and when victory is all but guaranteed. In such an instance, the addition of your individual vote will not affect the outcome, one way or the other, as was the case in Bosnia, where 99% said 'for'. Within days, that lovely multi-ethnic country was at war.

The result of that referendum, like the outcome of the 1990 elections, was almost definitely inaccurate. In November 1991, public opinion polls *"showed overwhelming majorities (in the range of 70 to 90 percent) against separation from Yugoslavia and against an ethnically divided republic".*[15] So either the methodology used by the pollsters was faulty, and/or the referendum itself was wrong. They cannot both be right.

Well, the referendum methodology is definitely at fault: a two-option question on a multi-option problem cannot produce the right answer, especially if both of the options listed are themselves extremes. An extreme, by definition, cannot represent the general consensus. *Ipso facto,* any two-option vote on two

13 Thompson, p 318.

14 Woodward, p 280.

15 *Ibid.*, p 228.

extremes is bound to be wrong! The thing that is so ridiculous in all this is that everyone knew there were more than two options. A number of possible compromise options had been discussed over the preceding months, not least the old but nevertheless good idea of a Yugoslav confederation. The people, however, were only allowed a choice of those two extremes. So yet again, anyone wanting to vote for a compromise was, in effect, disenfranchised![16]

We must recall the Northern Ireland story again, just for a moment, for a referendum can, sometimes, give a correct answer. In 1973, the ballot paper contained two extremes, so the answer was wrong. In 1998, there was a compromise; the answer in favour *might* mean it reflected the general consensus, but because it was the only compromise on offer, we still don't know for sure.

But to say the referendum in Bosnia accurately reflected the general consensus, even though the vote was another Stalinist 99% in favour, is just an absolute nonsense. Such a procedure is almost as non-sensical as an attempt to calculate the average age of a society by asking an either/or question based on two extremes: are you young or old? Regardless of the size of the majority, the answer is bound to be wrong!

* * * * * * * *

A third instance of this referendum madness relates to Kosova, another tale of western vacillation and human suffering. Kosova had been an autonomous region of Serbia, with a role in the joint presidency and so forth, since Tito's constitutional reform of 1974. Milošević put paid to all that in 1989, by re-integrating both Kosovo and Vojvodina back into one, centralist Serbia. But as we said earlier, the Europeans had said we would recognise *"internal borders"*; and Badinter had asked all who wanted to change their constitutional status to have a referendum. Kosova did exactly that.

On 22.10.91, in a land of roughly 90% Albanian, the turn-out was 87%; no surprises there. And there were no surprises either in the outcome: yet another Stalinist 99% voted for independence. Badinter did not say that's not enough, but he did decide the EC would not recognise that claim.

Kosovo, however, was not at peace. Ibrahim Rugova tried to pursue a policy of passive non-resistance, but others were getting impatient. In February 1996, the KLA came into being. Shortly afterwards, at the time of the pyramid crisis in Albania, a flood of weapons was smuggled across the Kosovan border. The situation inevitably deteriorated further. Eventually, peace talks were held at Rambouillet, and international diplomacy so-called tried to negotiate a settlement. Part of the package was to be a referendum in three years time.

---

16 In 1991, Serbia wanted to retain the FRY as presently constituted, that or, if other nations started to opt out, for the Serbian nation to opt out too. Macedonia and Bosnia meanwhile proposed a *"Yugoslav federation",* Slovenia and Croatia had already called for *"a loose confederation",* and the US had also suggested *"a confederation".* So there were definitely more than two options on the agenda, not only for the FRY as a whole - if only the FRY had itself held a referendum! - but also for each individual republic.

But we already knew what the answer would be. The previous referendum in 1991 had told us everything. By 1998/9, as long as the question was for something *roughly* Albanian - either an independent Kosova, or integration with Albania, or again, an even greater Albania - the Albanians were bound to win. (What they wanted *exactly*, however, would still remain uncertain! Majority voting does not work!) So the KLA signed. Milošević, on the other hand, was bound to lose. So he didn't sign. Therefore NATO bombed. Diplomacy is not what we thought it was; it is the long arm of 'pax Americana', and if you don't like what they demand, you will be forced into it.

Thoy bombeu and they bombed... but then they (or rather the Russians) renegotiated the agreement, and a referendum was no longer to be obligatory. Therefore, Milošević did sign. Therefore, the bombs stopped. Hundreds had been killed; thousands of Albanians had suffered even more ethnic cleansing; and all because of the mistakes of diplomacy.

NATO now says it wants the Serbs to stay, that it will enforce a multi-ethnic Kosova. Therefore, there *can* be no referendum! Will we ever learn? We might add, of course, that if the rules of international diplomacy were common to all conflict situations, the consequences of any signature refusals in Belfast would also have led to a few NATO bombs, either in Glengall St. and/or on the Falls Road, if not indeed in Downing Street and Leinster House!

* * * * * * * *

But back to majority voting. Some people now want Montenegro to have a referendum, thereby to break away from Serbia. Given the feelings in that divided republic, however, to hold such a divisive vote would again be unwise.

And what of consequences elsewhere? Certainly, if the Albanians in Kosova in Serbia are to be allowed to opt out, then what about the Albanians in Macedonia? As already noted, they boycotted Macedonia's full referendum in 1991. If, however, there was to be a vote in just the Albanian part of the Republic, doubtless the outcome would be different.

There will then be the question of the Bulgarians in Macedonia; of the Turks in Bulgaria; of the Kurds in Turkey, Iraq and Iran. And so it goes on and on, to Indonesia... and back again. There are the Hungarians in Vojvodina, for example, not to mention those in Romania. There are even more problems in the Caucasus, where referendums in Abhazia and Nagorno-Karabakh have done nothing to ease the pain, but that would need another book.

Maybe the worst consequence of any vote in Kosova, however, would be in Bosnia. For if an ex-autonomous part of Serbia can secede from Serbia, so too, surely, can an entity in Bosnia secede from Bosnia? Poplašen, the former president of *Republika Srpska*, said he wanted a referendum, (but he was later kicked out by the High Representative). Furthermore, that little entity has already had a number of referenda (see Annex I) which we would have wanted to recognise if but the answers had been more peaceful. Therefore, 'an ethnic peace' or referendum in Kosova could well cause yet another war in Bosnia!

The conclusion to all this is stark: in nearly all instances, referendums do not and cannot reflect the general consensus of society, because the choice available to the voters consists of only two options. Therefore, I repeat, the vote is not *'free'*. (The same is often true in majority votes in parliaments and councils.) To prove this point yet again, just in case any doubt still remains, let us take a simple dispassionate example, the Welsh referendum.

The question was devolution *D* or the *status quo S*, and the results indicated another cliff-hanger: in a 50.1% turnout, *D* got 50.3% to 49.7% for *S*. But *Plaid Cymru* had wanted independence *I* to be included on the ballot paper.[17] Well, if but 3% had voted *I* and not *D*, then *S* would have won, (assuming, that is, a majority/plurality vote).[18]

OK, so we know 51% voted for *D*. But we don't know whether or not 3% actually wanted *I*. In fact, maybe all 51% wanted *I* and maybe no-one wanted *D* at all. We simply don't know. The only thing we do know, for certain, is that Tony Blair wanted devolution and *not* independence; but he's not Welsh!

In similar fashion, the only thing we can say for certain as a result of the vote in Quebec, is that Parizeau wanted independence. Likewise in Croatia, even though the result was 90% in favour, the only thing we know for certain is that Tudjman was determined to secede.

Until people actually have the opportunity of voting in a multi-option ballot, all votes will be suspect if, that is, the issue in question involves more than two possible outcomes.

The multi-option (although still majoritarian) poll conducted in New Zealand was a distinct improvement, yet even this sort of poll tends to boil down to two or three favourites, not least because the media is indeed so disposed to simplify matters. In a points system of voting, however, where the outcome is dependent on *all* the points cast by *all* the voters on (one, some or) *all* the options, the outcome cannot be so easily predicted. Accordingly, any clear favourites would be less likely, and the campaigns for all options would in all probability be more fairly covered.

Finally, I should say that the above arguments against any use of the two-option vote apply in all circumstances, not only in national referenda, but also in parliaments and councils. The multi-option points system, the

---

17   In fact, they had argued for a four-option poll, while the Scottish Nationalists had wanted a three-option ballot. The latter poll was rather more clear cut, with 74% of a 60% turnout voting for devolution. By not putting independence on the ballot paper, however, the debate continues. Will Labour soon regret its majoritarianism in Scotland, I wonder.

18   If the voting mechanism had been a preferendum, the outcome would probably have been devolution. So the actual answer, *D*, *may* have been fair. Majority voting *can* sort of work, sometimes, but only if the correct question has been asked, and even then, only, as it were, by accident.

Borda preferendum count, is far more likely to yield *"a unique fairest outcome"*; what's more, *"it is the unique method... to minimise the likelihood that a small group can successfully manipulate the outcome".*[19] Most politicians have never heard of it. Instead, they continue to use majority voting, even though (or because) it is totally open to manipulation by those who set the question, namely, themselves.

---

19 Dummett, 1984, p 179 and Saari, p 14. I should add that both authors were referring to the Borda count, whereas here we are discussing the Borda preferendum. Given, however, that the latter is a development and an improvement, the quotes still apply.

CHAPTER 6

PEACE AGREEMENTS

*"Once your fall-back positions are published,
you have already fallen back to them."*

Abba Eban[1]

It wasn't all bad news in Northern Ireland. There was power-sharing in Dungannon, for example... though this might have been prompted by the fact that the electorate tended to choose a local council in which no-one side had an absolute majority. Be that as it may; those councils which chose to share the mayoralty, to ensure the committee chairs were distributed equally between the parties, to base any appointed bodies on relative party strengths, and so on, should nevertheless be supported.

The most notable absence in these arrangements lay in the fact that the average power-sharing council still took its decisions by majority vote. Proportionality could apply to all appointments, it seemed, but at the end of the day, on any one issue, there could only be one policy; therefore, apparently, they needed a majority vote. Such, it seemed, was the logic. The power-sharing arrangement still worked, of course, if all concerned chose to vote as it were by prior agreement; but any majority vote, and the whole power-sharing arrangement, was always very vulnerable to any change of mind.

In like fashion, as we said earlier, Tito also initiated a system of power sharing in Yugoslavia. He had no model on which to base his experiment, for apart from Switzerland, nearly every so-called democratic country practised no power-sharing at all. Nevertheless, this communist and supposed Stalinist introduced a measure of fairness which had not been seen before; he was, indeed, ahead of his times.

Apart from those already mentioned, there was one further weakness: *"The system of federal decision making by consensus and veto had no procedure for resolving differences between truly incompatible projects."*[2] Such a criticism could be made of almost any arrangement which allows interested parties the right of veto, a right which comes from, and is no less mythical than, its corollary, the right of majority rule.

---

1   See his *Diplomacy for the Next Century*, (see p 41fn), p 81.

2   Woodward, p 84. Tito had tried to insist on consensus - i.e., unanimity - in all fields of Yugoslavian life, and the first westeners to reject this methodology and opt instead for majoritarianism, were those of the IMF, in 1986; *ibid*, p 74. Were they, then, a cause of the subsequent wars? See also fn 8 on p 25.

Northern Ireland has long been administered by a form of national direct rule. Initially, that nation was Britain, but since the signing of the Anglo-Irish Agreement, the Irish government has also had a say. To-day, in theory, it is all changing, and a local form of power-sharing is due to take over the reins shortly, if but the politicians concerned can resolve certain outstanding issues like de-commissioning, the formation of the executive (and other problems, no doubt, yet to be highlighted). Until they do, of course, direct rule, apparently, must continue.

Mo Mowlem is doing her best to egg the process along. If anything, she is a referee, who blows a pretty fair whistle for any game Northern Ireland's politicians devise for themselves. The trouble with that approach, of course, is that these same politicians, because they are more oriented towards their sectional interests rather than to the general, tend to invent rules of veto and so forth, such as might well bring the game to a halt![3]

In Bosnia, the story is a little different. The Dayton Accord signalled the start of a period of international direct rule. The local politicians have a game to play, but it is Carlos Westendorp, the High Representative, who is the final arbiter on what the rules shall be. Furthermore, if the politicians themselves won't play, he picks up the ball himself... and scores! He has already taken a number of decisions, designing the new Bosnian flag, imposing a new common currency, and so on; and the current state of play is nil-nil-nil to the three main teams, and five or more to the ref! Furthermore, as was noted on p 50, he has sent one player off; Poplašen refused to play ball at all, so he was dismissed with aplomb, elected or not!

* * * * * * * *

In theory, in conflict management or conflict resolution, any mediator will try to find out what are the various preferences of those involved, so to identify that which will gain the greatest level of consensus of all of them. The Borda preferendum is a voting procedure which seeks to do exactly the same thing.[4]

Politicians, however, don't like to lose control of that agenda. Furthermore, they tend to regard any negotiations as a process in which they should

---

3   In majoritarianism, one side represents the majority and thinks it has *"the right to rule"*; the others, the minority, claim *"the right of veto"*. In such a milieu, many disputes end in alienation if there is a vote, or deadlock if there isn't. Each sides goes to the wire. Each refuses to reveal their compromise option, lest they lose their most favoured choice. And each refuses to reveal their *'fall-back position'*, to use Abba Eban's phrase, quoted at the start of the chapter.
    Such was almost the case during the Belfast Talks. On nearly every issue in dispute, each party refused to state their second preference lest in so doing they lost their first preference. Even on the very last morning, therefore, many details were still open to debate. Only by stint of some strong persuasion from both Downing Street and the White House did the participants agree, and the Good Friday Agreement was signed. As a result, the people then had their say. Humble folk that we are, we the people were allowed to utter one of only two words: yes or no.

4   In most cases, it will do just that, but see *Fallback Bargaining* by Steven J Brams, New York, 1998, p 10.

get as much as possible for their own sectional interests. They play hard ball, as they say, and they keep their cards close to their chest.

In the Belfast Talks, most participants sought to protect their own vested interests; and unfortunately, even when the referee should have known such rules were going to make the game pretty impossible, she usually preferred to agree with whatever they themselves had agreed to.

Some things, of course, they had to agree to. There was definitely to be some form of power-sharing, for public opinion would not have settled for anything less and, in any case, everyone agreed that majority rule in the new Assembly was just not on. In its place, they devised something called sufficient consensus, a phrase which originated in a South African context, and was later called parallel consent or consociational voting.

It works like this: the forum in question is divided into two, the two parts take a simultaneous vote, and if both parts say 'yes', then 'yes' it shall be. Needless to say, such a system is prone to the use of the veto. Furthermore, it is still very majoritarian, for if a majority of the majority or a majority of the minority prefers to say 'no', then there's an *impasse*. No wonder Paisley goes on so much about representing a majority of the majority. It is not, therefore, a very good system; it is, however, a vast improvement on any Westminster model.

Before we go on, I suppose we should put it into its historical context. Variations on this theme have been used in a number of jurisdictions, and the earliest known use was in the United Province of Canada, in 1840. In many instances, most especially in societies which are at peace with themselves, such as in Austria and the Netherlands, it has worked quite well. In countries of religious or racial division, however, in Cyprus and the Lebanon for example, it has not survived the test of time.[5]

As far as I know, the system was also devised by that sterling advocate of 99% majorities, Joseph Dzugashvili, better known to his Churchillian allies and communist comrades as Stalin. He had just taken control of Czechoslovakia where, he was told, the Czechs did not always get along with their Slovakian cousins. OK, said Joe, let both vote, and let's see if both agree. As a decision-making methodology, it worked very well throughout Stalin's lifetime... mainly because the Czechoslovaks themselves did not take *any* decisions in those days. As soon as they acquired their independence, however, the continued use of such a system created the *impasse* which led to the albeit reasonably peaceful collapse of their state.[6]

---

5   See *Consociation: The Model and its Applications in Divided Societies* by Arend Lijphart, writing in *Political Co-operation in Divided Societies,* edited by Desmond Rea, Gill and Macmillan, 1982.

6   I cannot recall the source of this particular gem of information, but maybe a different quotation will suffice. The following is taken from *The Soviet Electoral System* by Vitali Latov, Novosti Press Agency, Moscow, 1974, p 9. *"Every law must be passed by both. Should [they] disagree, the matter is referred for settlement to a conciliation commission."*

Though called 'parity of esteem', the Belfast Agreement gives only a 'parity of veto'. Either side can exercise a veto, if either thinks the opposite is asking for something too one-sided. And maybe, in 1998, that was as far as either side was prepared to go.

It was at least unwise, however, for the participants in those peace talks to not even consider either the historical precedents of consociational voting - the Czech example referred to above, or the three-sided version introduced into Bosnia in 1990 - or some of the more inclusive decision-making voting methodologies - the various multi-option procedures.[7]

Furthermore, it was deeply regrettable that, to make the whole thing workable, members to the new Assembly had to declare themselves to be unionist, nationalist, or "other". It was almost as if members were either 'this' or 'that'... or *"ethnically unclean"*. As noted earlier, sectarianism was thereby institutionalised.

At the same time, they decided, such a system could not be used province-wide, (even though the equivalent was what Badinter was asking for in Bosnia - see above, pp 47-8). This is because such a poll would require separate 'ethnic' electoral registers, the very thought of which surely offends all concerned with human rights.

Within the Assembly, however, they felt they *could* get away with it. Furthermore, as was only to be expected I suppose, the two big dogs, the two more moderate sectarian parties, made sure that they had more powers than any of those "others".

In some other particular aspects, the detail of the agreement was also rather unwise. For example, they decided that certain issues should be regarded as 'key', which is fair enough, but that such decisions could be taken by *two* forms of consociational voting. One mathematical formula consisted of at least two 50% majorities plus 50% overall; the second required at least 40% of each as long as there was an overall 60% majority.[8] There was therefore the possibility that a proposal could get the necessary weighted majority if one formula was used, even though it would fail under the second formula. It was, if anything, an agreement *"so that men might quarrel"*.[9]

There then comes the other question, of course: what is a key issue, and is the question of whether or not a question is key itself a key question? In other words, does the Assembly resolve this question of definition by

---

7   These include plurality votes, STV or the alternative vote, Condorcet criterion and the Borda count; see Emerson, 1998. After much persistence, a delegation from The de Borda Institute eventually met with Mr. Paul Murphy, MP, the Minister directly responsible for the Talks... yet he appeared to be unaware of even the existence of these methodologies.

8   See *The Agreement,* Strand 1, para 5 (d) (i) and (ii).

9   Lord Balfour's description of the English constitution.

simple or consociational majority vote? By leaving this matter of definition rather vague, they have created yet another potential argument, especially if more than a simple majority, but not as many as one and/or other consociational majority, are in favour.

Even on certain details of power-sharing, they deliberately left certain sections undecided, such as the number of persons to be elected onto the executive. There were to be between 6 and 10 ministers, they all agreed, and persons would be elected to the executive in d'Hondt[10] proportion to their party strengths obtained at the Assembly elections.

Once those results were declared, therefore, they fulfilled their agreement to argue, based on those numbers: some suggested the figure should definitely be 7 ministers, for that would mean 2 DUP and only 1 SF in the executive; others plumped for 6, for then both the DUP and SF would have just 1; a few wanted 9, for that would give the UUP 3 to every one else's 2; but predictably, they eventually settled for all 10 - UUP 3, SDLP 3, DUP 2 and SF 2 - regardless of expense! Once that was settled, they then had another argument, inventing 10 jobs and 10 ministries, where only 6 had been before!

* * * * * * * *

As stated earlier, Bosnia had set up a form of consociational government, before the war. In those days, the joint presidency consisted of 2 + 2 + 2 + 1, the 1 being an "other", a Yugoslav. After the war, under international guidance, they became more sectarian and deleted that singleton. The joint presidency was to consist of just the three persons, one from each national grouping.

That pre-war agreement, as we saw on p 38, as well as Tito's 'joint presidency' system of power-sharing (pp 33 and 53), also relied very much on the veto. So too does Dayton. In a word, it is all still very majoritarian. *"Each chamber shall by majority vote... select from its members one Serb, one Bosniac and one Croat..."* and *"All decisions shall be by majority of those present and voting"*.[11] Admittedly, there then follows a proviso to ensure that such a majority includes at least one third of the votes from each nationality. Furthermore, if the delegates of one of the three 'peoples' considers any proposal to be *"destructive of a vital interest"*,[12] they have to set up a Joint Commission, (as would those old Soviets), and it all gets very complicated.

Yet again, it seems, the participants at Dayton did not even think of using other forms of voting. Instead, they were stuck in that old majoritarian groove, dividing the country into two entities, so to give the rebel Bosnian Serbs a guaranteed majority in the *Republika Srpska*; and dividing the

---

10   See fn 7 on p 34.

11   The General Framework (Dayton) Agreement for Peace in Bosnia and Herzegovina, Annex 4, Article IV, para 3 (b) and (d).

12   *Ibid.*, (e).

other entity, the Federation, into ten separate cantons, so to give the Croats at least a few areas where they too would be in the majority.[13]

In local councils it's the same argument. Who has an absolute majority? And if the answer is no-one, who has a relative majority? In such councils as Travnik, where one group finished up with a majority of 1, such an obsession with majoritarianism is a recipe for just more conflict. Yet still the world persists.

* * * * * * * *

In Bosnia's case, It all started, I suppose, in 1992 in Lisbon, where they agreed to divide... (although Izetbegović soon changed his mind back again). There then followed all sorts of crazy plans, with lines all over the place, with some contiguous units and others disjointed, and huge potential for arguments as folks various wondered if they were to be in the majority or not, and if not, in whose. Little wonder, then, that such peace plans were not at all peaceful.[14]

Once the decision to effect a partition had been taken, it was perhaps inevitable that the final division would be into 3, or 2 twice. Bosnia is now divided, as was Ireland in the 1920s. It has taken us some 80 years to recover from the wounds, and it's not over yet. Hopefully, with the advent of modern television communications and an expanding EU, the recovery time in Bosnia will not be so long, despite the far greater level of suffering and her far more complicated history.

* * * * * * * *

Finally, we return to Kosova. The UN has now set up a Joint Council, in an effort to bring the Serbs and Albanians together. It is, in effect, another form of international direct rule, a UN Protectorate if you like, and we will be there for many years yet.

As already stated, majority rule will not work in Kosova, just as it cannot work in Northern Ireland, let alone in a three-cornered society as in Bosnia. Whether or not a (non-binding) voting methodology might be appropriate for any parliamentary forum in Kosova remains to be seen.

---

13 In Cantons 8 and 10, the HDZ got 80% and 60 % of the votes; in Canton 7, they got just 50%; and in Canton 2, they managed 55%. Needless to say, such results depend on the whereabouts of the cantonal borders; well, with but 20% of the Federation vote, the HDZ finished up with 40% of the cantons. The biggest Canton, based in Tuzla, where the HDZ has but 3% of the vote, has about ten times as many residents as the smallest, Canton 2 or Posavina, where the HDZ has that 55% majority. It was, yes, a fiddle. (1998 results).

14 The Vance-Owen Plan had ten separate provinces, with No 6 consisting of three separate bits. Owen-Stoltenberg suggested three sectarian areas, the Moslems having four bits, the Croats three, and only the Serbs having a contiguous concoction. And in similar fashion, the Contact Group suggested Srebrenica and Žepa should again be in a separate pocket, while Goražde and Višegrad would be joined in an extended finger.

What will certainly be required is some form of international arbitration in order to ensure a) that on any contentious issue, all the various parties' options become known to the other members, and b) that all concerned may then use some sort of decision-making methodology, facilitated by that arbitration, to identify the option most generally acceptable to all concerned. Such a methodology will almost invariably lead to a compromise which, in theory, is what politics is all about. So perhaps that's what is needed in Belfast and Bosnia as well.

ANNEX I

REFERENDA

*"Glancing at the peaceful little stalls where Christians,
Mussulmans and Jews mingle in business,
while each goes his own way to cathedral, mosque and synagogue,
I wondered if tolerance is not one of the greatest of virtues."*

L G Hornby[1]

Most of the referenda which took place in the former Yugoslavia are listed here. Some were only proposed, and these are shown in tint, while any national plebiscites on sovereignty in which the outcome was recognised by the EU are shown in reverse, (white on black).

{They also include one which was due to be held outside Yugoslavia, but nevertheless in relation to that sad land. And this Austrian attempt is added, if only to show how dangerous the very idea of a referendum could be, no matter in whose hands it lies. Do we allow the extremes to whip up emotions and force through measures such as immigration? Do we allow a majority of animal lovers to ban the eating of meat? Do we allow the non-smokers to ban all cigarettes? The railway commuters to ban cars? Is morality really to be subject to the dictates of a majority? It really is a most crude instrument!}

But back to Yugoslavia. For reasons unknown, the EC gave no consideration to the holding of a Yugoslav-wide referendum, though whether or not that would have done any good is debatable.[2] Gorbachev tried to stop the collapse of the Soviet Union by such a tactic in 1991, but despite the support of 77% of the vote - that's 105 million voters! - it still fell apart, for nothing can stop a movement whose time has come.

Secondly, the EU ignored the referenda held by groups not in recognised republics: those of the *krajina* Serbs in Croatia, of the Serbs in Bosnia, and of the Albanians in Kosova. If the last named had a case, as was later recognised in Rambouillet, then so too did the first. By 1999, of course, two of the three *krajina* had been ethnically cleansed by force, courtesy of Tudjman and the United States.

---

1   Quoted in Malcolm, 1996, p 168. Tolerance, of course, can rarely be expressed in any two-option referendum!

2   See footnote 16 on p 49. Doubtless, any such proposal would have been vetoed, not least by Slovenia, which had already vetoed any Yugoslav-wide elections, see p 36.

As far as those referenda which it did recognise are concerned, the results may perhaps be summarised by the following: *"the EC's insistence on referendums to legitimise these rights [to the ownership of historic lands], while accepting only some, provided the impetus... to create pure areas through population transfers and expulsions as a prelude to a vote."*[8]

The referendum is indeed a crude instrument. Its use in national plebiscites on sovereignty should be banned in all situations where the issue in question is controversial. Instead, any people seeking to secede should do so by reaching a consensus both amongst themselves within their new borders, and with their former compatriots and new neighbours in the old frontiers. Such can best be done by a multi-option process.

If we stick to the old two-option formula, which at the time of writing seems likely, I fear neighbours will continue to be enemies in the third millennium, especially in lands which are likely to change constitutionally: Indonesia and the Russian Federation, to name but two.

---

3   Woodward, p 271.

DATE	PLACE	ISSUE	Turn-out	For or Against	RESULT
. .88	FRY	const. amendments	n/a	n/a	Proposed, but vetoed by Slovenia & never took place.
01.07.90	Serbia	const. amendments	u/k	97%	Boycott by Kosovar Albanians.
17.08.90	*krajina*	autonomy	95%	99%	This vote set the *krajina* on a collision course with Zagreb.
.12.90	Serbia	presidency	u/k	86%	Milošević confirmed in power.
23.12.90	Slovenia	independence	94%	89%	a) a dispute over whether or not it meant secession; b) war.
.05.91	FRY	the future	n/a	n/a	Proposed, but vetoed by Slovenia & never took place.
12.05.91	*krajina*	stay in FRY	95%	90%	Ignored by Croatia, supported by Serbia...
19.05.91	Croatia[4]	independence	84%	93%	a) a Serb boycott b) war.
08.09.91	Macedonia	independence	72%	95%	Boycott by Albanians, 23%, and Serbs, 2%, of electorate.
09.11.91	'RS[5]	stay in FRY	85%	98%	Declared unconstitutional by others in Bosnia govt.
22.10.91	Kosova	independence	87%	99%	Not recognised by EU.[6]
25.10.91	Sandžak	autonomy	70%	99%	Organised by local Moslem National Council but not recognised by Serbia.[7]
01.03.92	Montenegro	stay in FRY	52%	75%	Moslem/Albanian boycott.
11.03.92	Bosnia	independence	63%	99%	a) Bosnian Serb boycott; b) war.

DATE	PLACE	ISSUE	Turn-out	For or Against	RESULT
11.10.92	Serbia	early vote	46%	95%	Declared invalid.[8]
.01.93	Austria	no immigrants	n/a	n/a	Proposed by right-wing Freedom Party.
15.05.93	RS	Vance-Owen	u/k	96%	No peace.
19.06.93	krajina	unity with RS	u/k	u/k	Ignored by Karadžić who does deal with Tudjman.[9]
28.08.94	RS	Contact group	u/k	90%	No peace.
. .98	RS	unity in Serbia	n/a	n/a	Thus far, only a proposal.
. .02	Kosova	Independence	-	-	Proposed at Rambouillet but later deferred.
. .	Monte-negro	Independence or stay in FRY	-	-	See 01.03.92 above, and page 50.

4   There was the second question on whether or not Croatia should remain in Yugoslavia, which was rejected by 92%; (see p 47).

5   *Republika Srpska* was not yet formally recognised, but the rebel Bosnian Serbs had established four 'krajina' in their bid to secede and, to further their campaign, they held a further two referenda on 21.12.91 and 09.01.92.

6   Later on, of course, in February 1999 at Rambouillet, this was all to change; see p 28 and pp 49-50.

7   These figures seem to be the subject of some dispute, and not least because the poll was disrupted. See RFE/RL Research Report of 3.11.92 by Milan Andrejevich. A similar referendum was held on 11.01.92 on the question of special status.

8   This was all part of a ploy by the then Prime Minister, Panić, to get rid of Milošević, but the wily old tyrant was saved by a rule which insisted on a minimum 50% turnout. Of such were the advantages to Milošević of that Kosovar boycott we mentioned, see p 36.

9   Woodward, p 310.

A BIBLIOGRAPHY

mainly for those, well versed in the Northern Irish problem,
who wish to become better acquainted with the Balkans.

The Agreement, Northern Ireland Office, 1998, is the full text of the Good Friday Agreement.

The General Framework Agreement for Peace in Bosnia and Herzegovina, 1995, is otherwise known as the Dayton Agreement.

ANDRIĆ, IVO

Bridge Over the Drina {first published as *Na Drina Cuprija*}, Harvill, 1994, a moving description of his native land by this deservedly famous Nobel laureate.

COHEN, LEONARD J

Broken Bonds - Yugoslavia's Disintegration and Balkan Politics in Transition, Westview press, 1995, does discuss electoral systems; there's hardly a word, though, on different decision-making processes!

DUMMETT, MICHAEL

Voting Procedures, OUP, 1984, is a most useful comparison. It is meant to be fairly untechnical, but I must confess, I found it quite heavy going.

Principles of Electoral Reform, OUP, 1997, describes the Quota Borda System (QBS). This one is more readily understood, with hardly any sums at all.

EMERSON, P J

A Bosnian Perspective, December Publications, 1993, relates his wartime experiences.

The Politics of Consensus, THE DE BORDA INSTITUTE, 1994, describes the only non-majoritarian decision-making voting procedure yet devised, namely, the Borda count as developed with partial voting into the Borda preferendum.

Beyond the Tyranny of the Majority, THE DE BORDA INSTITUTE, 1998, compares various decision-making processes and the more common electoral systems. It also suggests the principle of partial voting may be applied to QBS.

GLENNY, MISHA

The Fall of Yugoslavia, Penguin, 1992, is an accurate introduction to the Balkan conflict from this well-known former BBC correspondent.

The Balkans, Granta, 1999, a detailed and fascinating tome on a task perhaps too vast for us all.

HOLBROOKE, RICHARD *To End a War,* Random House, 1998, is a very readable account of how US foreign policy is based on a frightening combination of arrogance, ignorance, and bombs!

IDEA, *The International IDEA Handbook of Electoral System Design,* IDEA, 1997, gives an excellent summary of the various systems used throughout the world.

Democracy and Deep-Rooted Conflict: Options for Negotiation, IDEA, 1998, is printed in a confusing cacophony of colour, and is surprisingly ambivalent about voting methodologies.

LIJPHART, AREND *Electoral Systems and Party Systems,* Comparative European Studies, 1994, is an excellent comparison of current electoral systems. Alas, there is no equivalent on decision-making processes, for almost everyone uses that old wretched majority voting. He does, however, discuss two majoritarian forms of decision-making in his *Consociation: The Model and its Applications in Divided Societies,* (see p 55 fn).

MACLEAN, FITZROY *Josip Broz Tito - A Pictorial Biography,* MacMillan, 1980, is a wonderful insight into a remarkable individual. No wonder Tito is still so loved, and not only by Bosnians.

MALCOLM, NOEL *Bosnia - A Short History,* Papermac, 1994, (1996) and *Kosovo - A Short History,* Papermac, 1998, are two scholarly works for those interested in the detail.

ROHDE, DAVID *A Safe Area,* the desperate story of how we allowed Karadžić to massacre thousands of Moslems in Srebrenica.

SAARI, DONALD G *Basic Geometry of Voting,* Springer, 1995, a fiercely complicated work, but it too comes down in favour of the Borda count.

SILBER, LAURA, AND LITTLE, ALLAN, *The Death of Yugoslavia,* Penguin, BBC, 1995, a very well researched book from which was made a successful BBC documentary.

SINGLETON, FRED *A Short History of the Yugoslav Peoples,* Cambridge University Press, 1985, is useful for those who want to study the background to the conflict.

THOMPSON, MARK *A Paper House - The Ending of Yugoslavia,* 1992, is good but now a little dated.

WOODWARD, SUSAN *Balkan Tragedy - Chaos and Dissolution after the Cold War,* The Brookings Institution, 1995, is an excellent and detailed study, particularly good on the role of the USA, otherwise known as the 'international community'.

The following is a copy of the permit received by the author from the Bosnian Serb Army 'Press Centre' in Banja Luka; his translation is shown opposite. The basic form is shown in normal typeface, while the information added by the Banja Luka authorities is shown in italics.

VOJSKA REPUBLIKE SRPSKE
PRVI KRAJIŠKI KORPUS
Informativna služba
Datum   *18.01.*   199 *3* god.

PRESS
CENTAR

ODOBRENJE

U skladu sa Uputstvom za informisanje javnosti Vojske Republike Srpske, putem radija, televizije i štampe, odobrova sa posjeta vojnoj jedinici - territoriji *Banja Luka-Prnjavor-Derventa-Modriča-Brčko-Beograd.*

Ekipa novinara je u sastavu:

Ime i prezime	Lična isprava broj	MUP ili država
Peter Emerson, novinar	*Irish News*	*Irska*

Novinar putuje već danima biciklom, stigao je iz Zagreba - Okučana - Banjaluke i ide prema Beogradu.

Novinar putuju vozilom   *putuje biciklom*
Redakcija   *Irish News*

U toku boravka novinara, snimatelja i fotoreportera u jedinicama i na određenoj teritoriji upoznati ih šta je dozvoljeno za snimanje i informisanje a šta nije za javnost.

Novinskoj ekipi sa ovim odobrenjem pružiti neophodnu pomoć i stvoriti uslove za istinito i objektivno informisanje javnosti. Lica sa ovim odobrenjem dužna su se javiti vojnim i civilnim organima nadležnim za informisanje u svojoj zoni.

DOZVOLJEN RAD NA PRILOGU *Razgovor sa prolaznicima. Novinar poznaje srpski i ruski jezik i treba mu pružiti pomoć da nesmetano stigne na odredište i pokaže svetu da se i biciklom može slobodno pitovati kroz Republiku Srpsku. Nije dozvoljen samostalan rad na teritoriji i jedinicama bez prisustva nadležnih organa.*

Nije dozvoljen samostalan radu zonama odgovornosti bez prisustva nadležnih ovlaštenih lica. Za eventualna objašnjenja i dogovore javiti se na telefon 078/42-916 ili 11-606 ili 35-262 lokal 22-14.

NADLEŽNI STARJEŠINA

....
major Milovan Milutinović

My 'Odobrenje'

THE 'REPUBLIKA SRPSKA' ARMY
FIRST 'KRAJINA' CORPS
Information service

Date   *18.01.*   199 *3* year

PRESS
CENTRE

DECLARATION

In accordance with instructions laid down by the Republika Srpska Army for the broadcast of public information via radio, television or the press, approval is hereby granted for those journalists mentioned below to visit the following military commands and territories: Banja Luka-Prnjavor-Derventa-Modriča-Brčko-Belgrade.

Journalists Name and surname	ID	State
Peter Emerson, journalist	*Irish News*	*Ireland*

The above journalist is travelling the whole way by bicycle. He has come from Zagreb via Okučani to Banja Luka, and is travelling direct to Belgrade.

Means of transport	*bicycle*
Newspaper	*Irish News*

During the course of their deployment, the above journalists shall be informed that photographs are permitted in certain specified territories designated for this purpose whereas others are for the use of the general public.

This declaration demands that every assistance and the necessary conditions be granted to these journalists, for truthful and objective reporting. The holders of this declaration must identify themselves to the appropriate military and civilian authorities for all necessary information in their respective zones.

SUPPLEMENTARY PERMIT *Conversation with passers-by. The above-named journalist speaks Serbian and Russian.* **Every assistance must be given to him, so that he may travel freely and thereby show the world that it is possible to go across Republika Srpska even on a bicycle.** *He is not entitled to work independently in Republika Srpska without the necessary permits.*

The above mentioned is not permitted to any other work in the areas idenitified unless the relevant authorities are in attendance. For clarification or further information, call 078/42-916 or 11-606 or 35-262 ext. 22-14.

SENIOR OFFICER

....
major Milovan Milutinović

THE DE BORDA INSTITUTE

The de Borda Institute seeks to promote inclusive democratic procedures on all occasions of social choice, whether political or not, whether in relation to the election of representatives or concerned with the resolution of a dispute. Such voting procedures ensure that everybody contributes to the outcome and in such a way that no one faction wins everything but (almost) everyone wins something.

PURPOSES

The purposes of the Institute are sevenfold:

i) to promote the development and use of inclusive decision-making processes such as the Borda preferendum (subject if need be to a Condorcet count) whenever there are matters of controversy to be resolved by groups consisting of three or more members;

ii) to offer advice as to the advantages of the Borda preferendum over other decision-making voting methodologies;

and not withstanding the Institute's declared bias in favour of the preferendum,

iii) to facilitate any group wishing to use any decision-making voting procedure in common usage.

Given that the election of representatives is often crucial to any decision-making process, the Institute shall also seek:

iv) to promote the Borda preferendum, QBS and the QBS matrix vote as fair electoral systems;

to offer advice as to which inclusive electoral system should be used on which occasion;

vi) to demonstrate how these electoral systems are superior to most other known systems;

and again notwithstanding the Institute's declared bias in favour of these fairer systems,

vii) to facilitate any group wishing to use any known electoral system.

* * * * * * * *

THE DE BORDA INSTITUTE has given radio/TV interviews, presented lectures, conducted demonstrations and/or published articles and/or books in Albania, Armenia, Azerbaijan, Austria, Bosnia, Bulgaria, Canada, Croatia, Georgia, Germany, Ireland (North and South), Macedonia, Romania, Russia, Scotland, Serbia and The Ukraine.